"By skillfully guiding us through the emotio[...] helping us discover our attachment style, this book encourages growth while the child within feels lovingly held. It's connected, and it's a unique and enriching read."

> —**Irina Gladushchenko**, director of the International Energetic Healing Association, VET Trainer, and coauthor of the *Unfolding Journeys* anthology

"Jennifer Nurick has written a powerful and compassionate guide for anyone who struggles with anxious attachment. Drawing on both her personal and professional experience, she offers practical tools and strategies to help you heal from the wounds of insecurity, fear, and doubt. This book will help you transform your relationship with yourself and others, and embrace a more secure and authentic way of living."

> —**Scott Lyons**, holistic psychologist, mind-body medicine specialist, founder of The Embody Lab, and author of *Addicted to Drama*

"In *Heal Your Anxious Attachment*, Jennifer Nurick captures the essence of healing an attachment injury. 'It is the most important relationship I have—the one with myself.' Much like her Instagram presence, Jennifer helps her readers with gentle exercises and encouraging explanations, guiding each person beyond attachment 'adaptations' toward a more secure place within."

> —**Kelly McDaniel, MA, LPC**, author of *Ready to Heal* and *Mother Hunger*

"This is a compassionate book full of heart and healing. Jennifer has a deep knowledge of her field. She gives a very accessible account of how we form our attachment styles, and shows us practical and easy-to-follow processes which lead us toward healing. I can highly recommend this book."

> —**Jane Quayle, BCHC**, psychotherapist, and coordinator for the International Focusing Institute

"*Heal Your Anxious Attachment* is a must-read for anyone on a healing journey who is wanting to better understand themselves, and use that understanding to create a more meaningful life and deepen their relationships. With intuitively laid-out explanations for concepts that can be difficult to understand, paired with concrete and helpful exercises, this book forms a template for healing. Jennifer Nurick explores the cornerstones that form the foundation for healing in a way that is beautifully written, easy to understand, and covers a breadth of material, ideas, and exercises not seen in many other books."

—**Leah Katz, PhD**, clinical psychologist, and author of *Gutsy*

"This book speaks to the heart of anyone who's ever felt the pang of relational anxiety and self-doubt. The author doesn't just tell, she empathetically walks alongside you through every step, leading with her own vulnerability, wisdom, and therapeutic insight. This book doesn't merely explain theories; it resonates on a deeply emotional level, providing holistic, trauma-informed strategies to guide you toward healing and secure connection."

—**Matthias Barker, LMHC**, cofounder and CEO of the Trauma Institute

Heal Your Anxious Attachment

Release Past Trauma,
Cultivate Secure Relationships &
Nurture a Deeper Sense of Self

Jennifer Nurick, MA

REVEAL PRESS
AN IMPRINT OF NEW HARBINGER PUBLICATIONS

Publisher's Note

This publication is designed to provide accurate and authoritative information in regard to the subject matter covered. It is sold with the understanding that the publisher is not engaged in rendering psychological, financial, legal, or other professional services. If expert assistance or counseling is needed, the services of a competent professional should be sought.

NEW HARBINGER PUBLICATIONS is a registered trademark of New Harbinger Publications, Inc.

New Harbinger Publications is an employee-owned company.

Reveal Press
An imprint of New Harbinger Publications, Inc.
5720 Shattuck Avenue
Oakland, CA 94609
www.newharbinger.com

Cover design by Amy Shoup

Acquired by Georgia Kolias

Edited by Gretel Hakanson

Library of Congress Cataloging-in-Publication Data on file

Printed in the United States of America

26	25	24								
10	9	8	7	6	5	4	3	2	1	First Printing

Contents

Introduction

You are not broken, in need of fixing. You are deeply hurt, in need of care.

—Arielle Schwartz, *The Complex PTSD Workbook*

You have been drawn to this book because you are ready to heal your anxious attachment and the shame, confusion, disconnection, and pain accompanying it. Anxious attachment pain may be triggered in a variety of ways, but the experience is familiar. Let's say your partner unexpectedly receives a text from their ex. Your heart pounds, and your mind starts racing at a hundred miles an hour: *How long have they been talking? Has he been cheating on me? Is he going to leave me?* You are flooded with emotion. When you ask about the message, you are already shouting because you have assumed the worst. Your partner responds defensively and dismisses (rather than reassures) you. You threaten to leave the relationship. This is the last thing you want, but you seem to have no control over your behavior and can't calm down.

Afterward, you panic, terrified that your partner is going to break up with you for your "crazy" behavior. You feel confused and ashamed about how you reacted. *I'm messed up; there's something wrong with me. I'm going to be alone forever.* These thoughts are like a knife to your heart, damaging your sense of self-worth and ability to trust yourself. You just need to be reassured that your partner is faithful, that they love you, and that you are safe in the relationship.

Sometimes you receive this reassurance. Sometimes you do not, which leaves you in a repeating cycle of feeling out of control, even like you are crazy. Know that you are not crazy, that you are not alone in this experience, and that you are welcome here in this safe space with me. I hope this book will help you understand and break these painful cycles. You can create a strong sense of self-worth, self-trust, and self-confidence to experience life and relationships from a place of calm and connectedness. You are ready. You deserve this.

As we begin, know this: Your anxious attachment is a healthy adaptation to a confusing situation. It results from your first experiences with love and connectedness from your early childhood. This means you make sense. To emphasize this, in this book, wherever possible, I have changed the phrase "anxious attachment" to "anxious adaptation." Doing this emphasizes the root cause of this phenomenon as an *adaptation*, not a diagnosis or disorder.

Imagine that as a child you were like a seed, landing on the forest floor, full of potential. A seed will grow according to the light, moisture, and nutrients it receives. It grows around the roots of the other trees and finds pockets of nourishment. You were the same, quickly learning to adapt your behavior to your surroundings to stay safe and survive. These adaptations you made then will influence the rest of your life. They become the lens through which you perceive and operate in the world.

Attachment adaptations are the result of experiencing different kinds of trauma during your childhood. They include what some have called "big-T trauma," such as abuse, neglect, domestic violence, living in a war zone. They also encompass "small-t trauma," like ongoing bullying, feeling unloved, repeatedly being told that you are stupid, or living with an adult where there is little emotional connection. Don't dismiss small-t trauma as not being "real trauma," small-t traumas build up, like a thousand tiny paper cuts, and significantly impact your emotional development and the adult you have become. Children "can be wounded in multiple ways: by bad things happening, yes, but also by good things not happening" (Maté and Maté 2022, 23). When you are in the moment, experiencing an anxious attachment adaptation, and frustrated with yourself, it's likely you are unaware of the unresolved childhood trauma that sits behind it.

I know this pain well because I have lived it myself. I grew up in an area peppered with alcoholics, drug users, and domestic violence, mixed in with the friendly neighbors trying to do their best to live a good life. We all knew the houses that were safe and the ones that weren't. In my home, I knew things weren't right. But because it looked better than others and because I was frequently told how lucky I was, I was convinced things were okay. Still, a nagging feeling wouldn't leave. There was something about it that was not okay.

Only as an adult could I see that for most of my childhood, my dad suffered with mental health issues. As a child, I was confused: *Why didn't he love me? What was wrong with me? Why wouldn't he speak to me for days at a time?* I learned to be vigilant around him, to watch for signs of upsetting him, and to moderate my behavior. I learned that love was not freely given, that love was conditional, and that something about me was unlovable. My anxious adaptations around relationships grew out of this fertile soil.

After I left home, as a young adult, I continued a pattern of landing in relationships where I felt anxious. I fell deeply in love with a man from a strict religious tradition. We wanted to get married, but both he and his parents wanted me to convert. The subtext said: "We will try to break you up unless you convert. If you do what we want, you will be accepted (maybe)." It was a repeating cycle of unprocessed childhood pain.

On top of that, my partner was aloof and often felt distant, so I found myself feeling anxious. Again, I was being presented with a situation where something about me was unlovable. My mind would reason that it was because I was not the right religion, but my body and heart couldn't feel it. As he mediated between his family and me, I felt alone and betrayed, without anyone to support me. This is where I abandoned myself without knowing it. I was so disconnected from my core self and afraid of being rejected further that I struggled to set boundaries to protect myself.

This made me mentally, emotionally, and spiritually ill. Through the worst year, I cried almost daily, as I was increasingly in touch with feelings that I thought I'd buried along with my childhood. I found it challenging to regulate myself; I didn't recognize myself and knew that I needed some help.

This book distils many years of my personal and clinical work; it is a roadmap to the work. As a psychotherapist and energetic healer, I have walked with thousands of people on their journey of healing the anxious attachment adaptation and finding their way to secure love of themselves and others. While I primarily work with women in heterosexual relationships, everything presented in this book applies equally to all sexual orientations and gender identities.

Within this book, you will learn about the anxious adaptation, how it is formed, and what it looks like in action as you embark on your healing journey. You will learn holistic, trauma-informed, body-based methods, mindfulness techniques, and "parts" work. The first half of the book takes you on a journey of coming home to your self in body, mind, emotions, and spirit so you can develop what I call an *internal secure attachment*. The second half explores how you can learn to be in intimate relationships, where we unpack co-regulation, triggers, boundaries, communication, and other meaningful connections to help you build secure, flourishing relationships.

This book is intended for you whether you have thought about therapy but have not yet made the leap, or if you are currently engaged in psychotherapy and plan to use the book as an adjunct. This book is not a substitute for therapy. All attachment adaptations were forged in the fire of early childhood relationships. They are interpersonal adaptations, so being in the presence of an attuned, compassionate, and trauma-informed therapist will expedite your healing process and allow for reparative experiences.

Moving into secure attachment is a journey. I like to think of this healing journey as the quintessential hero's journey, where the hero embarks on an adventure, faces challenges, and returns as a changed person (Campbell 1949). The healing journey is not for the fainthearted. It is for those ready to look within who are prepared to observe and challenge the old programming and gather the tools needed on the road back to self.

A cyclone may have hit your life and brought you to this book, as the beginning of your quest. As with any hero's journey, there will be moments of fear and pain, out of which grow the gifts of your empowerment and secure attachment. On this journey, bring the gifts of *curiosity* and *kindness.* Curiosity, because it is an antidote to self-judgment. Kindness, because it stops you from punishing yourself.

Know that you are not alone on this journey. An estimated 58 percent of people have one of the three insecure attachment adaptations: anxious, avoidant, and disorganized (Konrath et al. 2014). It is possible to move toward secure attachment as an adult. I invite you to reflect on how far you have already come and how resilient you are. Right now, as you read these words, you have the power to choose how you move forward with this precious life.

Gathering Your Resources for This Journey

When therapists talk about "resources," they are referring to all the skills, tools, abilities, and relationships available to you that help you regulate your nervous system and bring you back to a place of calmness, and help build resilience. I suggest you keep a journal as you work through this book. There is no "right way" to do journaling. Use it in whatever way feels supportive to you. Think of your journal as a private space to chat with your best friend without judgment, a place to reflect and organize your thoughts and feelings and help integrate the shifts you will experience. You may like to use a journal with space for drawing because some of what you want to record or explore may be more symbolic or come in images. There will also be reflections and experiences from the writing prompts in this book.

A fantastic way to enjoy this journey is with a friend. You might know someone who also struggles with anxious tendencies and choose to meet up once a week to discuss a chapter and even lead each other through some of the exercises.

The exercises in this book are structured to take your body, mind, and spirit on a holistic journey, so you are encouraged to do them as you come to them and not proceed in the book until you can do them, rather than return to the exercises later. I have recorded many of the exercises as downloadable audio files that you can access for free on my website http://www.psychotherapycentral.health/anxious-attachment. Many people find something comforting and supportive in hearing a caring voice guide them, but everyone is different, and if this doesn't work for you, you could record the practices on your phone and then listen to your voice lovingly guide yourself.

Every exercise you do in this book is an *experiment*. Some of these experiments will become resources, an additional skill or ability that aids self-regulation and helps keep you in your social engagement system (aka "ventral vagal," which you'll learn about in chapter 6). Other exercises may not become resources for you, and that's okay. I invite you to use what works and leave what doesn't suit you. Many instructions will ask you to close your eyes; this allows most people to go into a deeper self-reflective state because some outside stimulus is blocked. But closing your eyes may be uncomfortable. If that is the case, I invite you to lower your gaze and soften your focus for the exercises.

Working with my body, mind, emotions, and spirit has helped me create a stronger sense of self, self-worth, and self-trust. I have much clearer boundaries and can communicate them more skillfully than before. I feel connected to my core needs and values and have learned how to reference these needs before taking care of everyone else around me. Even though I still get triggered occasionally, I can return to a felt sense of calm faster and tend not to get stuck in anxious reactions for days at a time like I used to. That's why I proudly share this work with my clients, students, and you, my reader.

Despite the early difficulties in my relationship, I married the man I mentioned above, and we have two beautiful, empathic, and joy-filled children. We have both grown and changed since our wedding; we have held at the forefront of our hearts the desire to move into deeper intimacy with one another, even when it is difficult. Through the vehicle of our relationship, more of myself has been revealed to me, and we have developed a secure relationship that we both value and, with it, more secure individual tendencies.

An unexpected by-product of this healing work has been a deep sense of inner peace and connectedness that extends to all living beings, which has fueled a desire to serve others. We commonly do the healing work on ourselves first and are drawn to help others as a result. Allow yourself the time you need for your own healing.

It might be that your anxious adaptation is revealed to be one of your biggest gifts, as it was for me; my greatest pain pulled me into a future I could only have imagined. Know that I am with you every step of the way on this journey, cheering you on. You can do this.

CHAPTER 1

Your Anxious Attachment Is an Adaptation

He walks in the room, and you know something is wrong. He's angry. Have you done something? Is he angry with you? What can you do to fix it? You act casual, but you are watching him like a hawk in your peripheral vision. He says he had a bad day at work and his boss is being an idiot. He doesn't look at you while he's speaking. He's making some tea. He feels distant. You feel tense. You can't relax until you feel closer to him. You don't feel safe. You try to talk to him about his day at work, but he says he doesn't want to talk about it and just wants to watch the news and zone out. You follow him to the TV room. You watch TV, but you are waiting for a sign that it is safe to get closer. You make some comments about the news to see how he responds. He seems more relaxed. You reach over to squeeze his hand. He squeezes your hand in return. You didn't realize until that moment just how stressed you had been. A wave of relief washes over you. The relationship is safe, and so you are safe. Exhale.

When you have the anxious adaptation, scenes like this are typical. You might have noticed in intimate relationships that you tend to be hypervigilant about your partner's mood and how close you feel to one another. You are likely to be hyperaware of moments when your partner seems to pull away and find that you have a strong reaction and struggle to calm down until they feel close again. In those moments, you need reassurance that the relationship is safe and that they love and care for you. In the back of your mind, you are wondering if they will stay with you. You feel that they are somehow better than you. It's so difficult to believe that they care for you. No matter how much they tell or show you, there's always a nagging doubt that they will find something unlovable in you and leave. And that would be the most devastating thing. To be left. To have your fears confirmed. You'll do anything to prevent that. This is where you betray yourself in big and small ways. It might be saying something is okay when it is not or always putting their needs before yours. You might also start to feel like you can't survive without them, that they are the only good thing in your life, becoming emotionally dependent.

Know that you are not alone in this experience. This is the impact of your anxious attachment adaptation.

Attachment Theory, the Dance of Love

Attachment theory emerged from the work of psychiatrist and psycho-analyst John Bowlby (1969, 1988) and has been built on by neuroscientists and social psychologists. All children have an inbuilt attachment system that drives them to stay close to their caregivers to help them survive in an unpredictable and sometimes dangerous world. The goal of this attachment system is a "sense of felt security" (Mikulincer and Shaver 2016, 12). You can relax when you feel safe and know that your caregiver is close and responsive. If you are unsure if they will be there in the way you need, part of you must remain on high alert, anxious.

We develop this sense of felt security from the experience of being attuned to. *Attunement* happens when someone is aware of your physical and emotional needs and is lovingly responsive to them. You will have developed a secure attachment style if you have received *good enough* attunement from your attachment figure as a child. Picture a ten-month-old in their bouncer who starts to get bored or hungry. They moan and move their arms and legs, looking toward their mother. The mother sees this gentle call for attention, approaches, and lifts them out of their bouncer while asking what they might need with a loving voice. This is attunement. The infant doesn't need to escalate, to start to cry or scream, because they have been attended to.

What helps us create secure attachment? Researchers have found protection, attunement, soothing, expressed delight in the child, and encouragement to be core factors in creating a secure attachment (Brown and Elliott 2016). When these five conditions are met enough of the time, a secure attachment is formed, and as a result, we grow healthy and supportive ideas about ourselves and others. If there was insufficient attunement, you would have formed one of the three insecure attachment styles: anxious, avoidant, or disorganized.

Your anxious attachment adaptation is a logical and natural response to inconsistent, unpredictable, or overly anxious parenting, especially by your primary caregiver. You might have grown up with a traumatized mother who was terrified of you being hurt in the way she was, so she was overprotective and smothering, limiting your natural desire to explore the world. Or perhaps you had an inconsistent caregiver—sometimes validating and emotionally available, but sometimes overwhelmed by working three jobs, caring for a sibling who needs a lot of attention, or managing an abusive partner. This causes you to become hypersensitive to their behavior, tone of voice, and change in mood, as you try to get your needs met.

While you make space to acknowledge how it was for you in your childhood, it is important to note that the intention here is not to blame your parents or make them wrong for everything they did or didn't do. It is to recognize where the patterns have come from, for the patterns to make sense, given some of the things you did and didn't experience in your childhood. These experiences of connection and disconnection created embedded patterns of relating and attaching, which built the foundation for your future intimate relationships.

Forming a Relationship Template

Attachment patterns are created through repeated relational interactions. Imagine that as a child, something happens and you feel scared. You go to your caregiver for safety and support. The caregiver is not available. Maybe they are working or caring for other children and shoo you away. Perhaps they have depression or a physical illness and struggle to care for themselves. You learn not to go there for safety and support. Then what? Generally, you would have used one of two strategies. The first is hyperactivating (anxious)—thoughts and feelings that make you want to get closer to your caregiver—which might look like watching your carer's every move to try to work out when and how to get your needs met or becoming more distressed and demanding. Alternatively, you might have used deactivating (avoidant) strategies—thoughts and feelings that compel you to move away from the caregiver—which might look like ignoring the caregiver and denying that they have any impact on you. You start to ask for less and suppress your needs (Mikulincer and Shaver 2016). For both the anxious and the avoidant styles, you learn that you cannot rely on a relationship with another person to provide you with the soothing or protection you need.

These interactions form a template for what Bowlby referred to as your "internal working model," a mental representation, or template, of what you expect to happen in relationships based on what you have experienced (Bowlby 1969). You then use this model to assess how relationships are as an automatic knowing. These models include how you see yourself and how you expect others to respond to you.

Children are wired to survive. You might like to take a moment and thank your nervous system and yourself as a child for being adaptable enough to survive.

Attachment in Adulthood

Just as children have a survival instinct to stay connected to their caregiver, research shows that this continues into adulthood with a drive to have an intimate attachment figure (Hazan and Shaver 1987). A growing body of research demonstrates the similarity of the child-caregiver relationship to the adult-couple relationship (Zeifman and Hazan 2016). Researchers have explored the patterns of infant-caregiver separation and found that intimate partner relationships follow a similar pattern during periods of separation.

By the time we are fully grown adults, we already have an imprint of how intimate relationships work based on our childhood experiences.

These form a template for our adult relationships, whereby we will tend to expect what we received as a child and will have an automatic pull to respond in the same way we did as a child.

Thinking in Terms of Relational Distance

The easiest way to think about attachment patterns in adulthood is in terms of relational space and connection. Securely attached people like some overlap and some independence, creating interdependence. Avoidantly attached people like more relational space and less connection and struggle to find a place to overlap; it feels unsafe to them. Anxiously attached people like a lot of overlap and connection; too much distance feels unsafe.

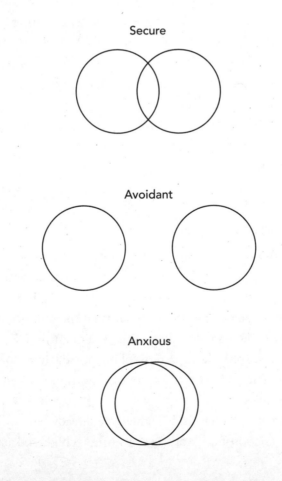

Do You Have an Anxious Attachment?

As you answer the following questions, consider a recent or current significant relationship. Using your journal, work through the statements below (Fraley, Waller, and Brennan 2000; Levine and Heller 2010; Heller 2019) and rate them according to the following scale:

True: 3 points

Sometimes true: 2 points

Not at all true: 1 point

1. Do you tend to get attached to a new partner quickly and find it difficult to keep perspective?

2. When you get upset, do you find it difficult to calm yourself down and feel that you need others to calm you?

3. In a relationship, do you tend to put your partner's needs before your own?

4. Do you feel that your partner doesn't care about you as much as you care about them?

5. Do you find that you are highly attuned to your partner's mood?

6. Do you find yourself yearning for emotional validation (to have your emotions understood and accepted by your partner)?

7. Once you sense something is wrong in the relationship, do you feel compelled to fix it, even to your detriment?

8. Do you have a pattern of over-giving in relationships and then feeling resentful?

9. Is it difficult to feel your partner's love when they express it in different ways?

10. Do you tend to become highly reactive and distressed during conflict?

11. Do you frequently worry about your relationship ending?

12. Is it difficult for you to know where your boundaries are?

13. Do you worry about being abandoned?

14. Is it challenging to be alone? Do you find being alone triggers strong emotions?

15. Do you worry that when your partner gets to know you, they won't like who you are?

Notice if you have a lot of 1, 2 or 3s. If you have a lot of 1s, you are likely to be more on the avoidant end of the attachment spectrum. If you have a lot of 2s, you are more secure in your attachment style. If you have a lot of 3s, you are more anxious in your attachment style.

The Challenges of the Anxious Adaptation

Research has shown that there are three core challenges of the anxious adaptation. First, the current template of how you see yourself in relation to others often leaves you feeling less worthy than your partner and wondering when they are going to find out and leave you. We consciously work on this template in chapters 2 through 6. The second challenge is that of *regulation*, of calming yourself down once you have become upset. We discuss this in detail in chapter 6. Third are the anxious patterns that you see when you enter an intimate relationship: the anxiety that they are going to leave, noticing signs of rejection, wanting a lot of reassurance, feeling hypervigilant around them, putting their needs before your own, pushing them for a response and validation, and when you don't get it, pushing harder, which pushes them further away. We cover all of this and more in chapters 7 through 11.

What Is It Like to Be Securely Attached?

When an infant is securely attached, they have experienced a caregiver who is attuned and present—*often enough*. They have learned that they are worthy of attention and love so have formed positive internal templates of themselves and others. This translates into securely attached adults who:

- are comfortable being alone

- can acknowledge internal distress and manage their feelings in a healthy way (self-regulate)

- can identify emotions and share them with others

- communicate openly and honestly

- have a positive image of themselves and others and know that they are loveable

- assume that others mean well most of the time

- tend to show respect and gratitude toward their partner

- tend to be open and honest and to trust the other person when they start dating

- are less likely to have one-night stands and report mutual initiation and pleasure from sex (Feeney 2016)

- are comfortable with connection, intimacy, and vulnerability, and their partner's vulnerability

- have a supportive, caring inner voice

- are able to compassionately self-reflect

- know how to be interdependent—are able to find a balance between being connected with another person and being alone.

A secure relationship feels warm and safe, with room for exploration, adventure, and joy. There is a general sense of both people caring about one another and being available and supportive. Both people expect to be valued and loved because this is what they are used to. Securely attached people find it easy and desirable to be in a relationship and find a balance between being independent and being connected—interdependent. They can understand their partner's experiences and listen to complaints without it affecting their self-esteem, and they can be vulnerable and hold space for their partner's vulnerability.

Securely attached people can feel activated (experience strong emotions and body sensations) and still identify what they need and reach out for it in the relationship. When they receive what they have asked for, they can accept what has been offered and feel calm again. They have strong self-esteem and can self-regulate; this means when emotions come up, they notice the feelings and have healthy ways to cope with them and self-soothe.

Being with Someone Safe and Loving (Remembering a "Secure" Experience)

This exercise teaches you to amplify and draw on past experiences that have felt safe and connected. Research has shown that drawing on these experiences leads to behavior change where we act more securely (Hudson, Chopik, and Briley, 2020). A guided audio recording of this exercise is available at http://www.psychotherapycentral.health /anxious-attachment.

Take a moment to think back to a time when you felt loved and safe in the presence of another living being. It might be a relative, friend, teacher, or pet.

Let yourself go back to that time in your imagination. Where were you? Notice what you can see, hear, and smell. What did it feel like to be in their presence? What sensations do you feel in your body?

Notice what kind of contact you would like to have. What kind of touch would make you feel the most loved, connected, and safe?

Allow yourself some time to be in this space, noticing their desire to be with you, to protect you, and their love for you.

You might like to thank them for their presence in your life and for the special moments you shared.

When this feels complete, gently bring your awareness to your whole body. Gently rub your hands on your thighs and notice the friction. When you are ready, open your eyes and look over one shoulder, noticing a few things in the room as you do so. Then look over the other shoulder until you feel you are back in your space and grounded.

Take a moment to journal about your experience with this exercise.

Attachment Research

Research shows that secure attachment is associated with "almost every positive index of mental health and general well-being outlined in the social sciences" (Johnson 2019, 10; Mikulincer and Shaver 2016).

Insecurely attached infants are more likely to report illness thirty years later than those who were securely attached, and insecure attachment is linked to higher rates of obesity in US preschool-aged children (Anderson and Whitaker 2011). In the words of Kelly McDaniel (2021, 63), counselor and author, "hunger and bonding are inextricably biologically linked." When we are not receiving the bonding and love that we require, it is natural that we try to fill this void in another way; food is one of the ways. Higher attachment security is linked with more success in intimate relationships, including friendships, less depression, and better memory and attention (Hudson, Chopik, and Briley 2020).

The good news is that research shows that your attachment style can change over time (Hudson, Chopik, and Briley 2020). It is possible for you to create new templates of how you see yourself and others and to develop new patterns of connection (Egeland, Jacobvitz, and Sroufe 1988). Creating secure attachment is a journey—perhaps the most challenging and exciting journey you will ever go on. It is a journey of deep healing and of coming home to your core self. It is a journey of love, of falling in love with yourself first and with your partner next. You begin this process of falling in love with yourself by first paying attention to yourself in a new way, by becoming more present and grounded.

Present and Grounded

Have you ever noticed that anxiety takes you out of your body and into your head where you can't seem to focus on anything except the anxiety? For this reason, I'm going to teach you how to practice becoming more present and grounded in quiet moments, so when you are in a wave of anxiety, you will be able to come out of it more easily.

As you read this, how present are you? Are you trying to rush through the book to get your problems solved? Are you distracted by things going on around you? Are you aware of your surroundings? Learning to increase your level of presence and groundedness (felt sense of being connected to the earth) increases your sense of safety. Usually, when you are activated (or triggered), you have stopped feeling safe, so learning to increase your sense of presence and groundedness is a key to mastering your reactivity.

One of the most powerful exercises to become present and grounded in the here and now is to practice noticing your surroundings through your five senses. In this exercise you are going to try two different experiments to feel grounded. I like to use experiments because I find in my practice that what works for one person does not always work for another person, and often when you find the best tool for you, you know it. You are your own best teacher.

This is available to listen to at http://www.psychotherapycentral. health/anxious-attachment.

Present

Look up from the book for a moment and let your eyes wander around the space you are sitting in.

See. What can you see? You might notice large objects and more minor details as you look around the room, and you might notice different colors. Just notice what you see without judging or starting an inner dialogue about anything.

Hear. What can you hear? Listening to the different layers of sound around you, notice their subtle differences.

Smell. What can you smell? Notice the distinct smells around you. They might be faint, and you may have to pay close attention to them.

Taste. What can you taste? Take a moment to notice what you can taste. You might move your tongue gently to get a better sense of what tastes are present.

Touch. Notice what you can feel on your skin. What do your clothes feel like on your body? Can you sense a difference between the different items of clothing in texture or tightness?

Grounded

Experiment 1. Points of connection. When you are ready, take your attention to the points of connection between yourself, the chair, and the floor. Allow yourself to feel the support of the chair and the floor. Notice how some contact points have more pressure resting on them than others. Choose one point that has a strong pressure and rest your focus there. You may find your mind start to drift. This is natural. Gently bring it back to your point of focus, knowing that you are increasing your capacity for awareness and attention every time you do this.

Experiment 2. The tree. Sitting upright for this experiment, imagine your torso is like a tree trunk. Exhale and imagine sending big thick roots into the earth below. When you inhale, bring the breath and earth energy up into your torso. Exhaling again, send the breath down into the earth, imagining the roots going deeper and becoming wider. As you inhale, breathe the energy up, and exhale, taking it down further, deeply connecting you into the earth. Inhale and with the next exhale, thousands of tiny root networks shoot off your main root, anchoring you into the earth and connecting you with the root networks of other strong trees in the soil. You might become aware of tree root networks throughout the soil and become anchored in that network and strengthened by their presence. Continue this practice for around three minutes.

Journaling

Take some time now to write down your experience of these practices. Is your mind calmer or more distracted? Does your body feel more or less grounded? How do you know? Which of the two grounding experiments did you prefer? What was it about that practice that made you feel more grounded?

These exercises are applications of mindfulness. Every time you do them, you increase your ability to be present and grounded, and you teach your body what it feels like to recognize that you are safe. I recommend doing your preferred exercise once a day for five minutes. You will notice that your practice will change with time, becoming richer, and that it will start to enrich your life in general.

Noticing

Noticing is the subtle art of reconnecting with your inner experience and developing an important part of yourself that I call the "observer" self. The benefit of cultivating this part of you is the ability to have some distance and an attitude of compassion when you are experiencing strong feelings and thoughts. Noticing is different than thinking in that you are not judging or examining; instead, you are being the nonjudgmental, compassionate observer of yourself. When I notice myself get angry and feel a wave of heat moving through my torso, there is a slight distance between "me" and the emotions and sensations. I think, *Wow, I'm feeling furious right now. I can feel this intense wave of heat moving through my torso.* I have a sense of being in my body and feeling the sensations and being an internal observer of my experience. This usually reduces the sense of being overwhelmed by the experience.

The main aim of this practice is to begin the process of listening to your body. You will start to notice your thoughts, feelings, and body sensations at any given moment. This helps with one of the core challenges of the anxious adaptation: differentiating those feelings and sensations without becoming overwhelmed by them. Over time, this practice builds your capacity to experience a range of emotions and bodily sensations and increases your general resilience.

It is difficult to judge yourself when you are "noticing" with child-like curiosity. If you cannot remember feeling that way, notice with a sense of kindness toward yourself or think of your best friend and how you would respond to them.

Here's an example of what noticing might look like after reading this chapter: *Wow! After reading about the anxious attachment style, I notice a sense of relief and hope. I feel a sense of excitement, expansion, and warmth in my chest.* (The identified feelings include relief, hope, and excitement. The identified sensations are expansion and warmth and a location: in the chest.)

And there is something else. Ummm. What is that?... Ah, I'm noticing grief for the younger me. I feel it in my arms, like I want to reach up for a supportive and loving mother. Yes, there is an intense feeling in my arms, like heat, and kind of achy.

I make space for both the grief and the hope and excitement. I can hold both in my body and my mind.

Bringing your curiosity and kindness to the forefront, take a moment to practice noticing sensations in the body and naming emotions and feelings as they arise. This practice is available to listen to at http://www.psychotherapycentral.health/anxious-attachment.

When you feel ready, gently turn your awareness to your body. Notice the sensation of your body touching the chair. Notice where there seems to be more and less pressure. Notice, without judgment, how your body is feeling right now. What sensations are present after reading this chapter and thinking about your anxious adaptation?

Just notice whatever felt sensations come up without having to move away from them—you are simply noticing and naming.

You might not feel anything as you sense into your body. Be patient. Notice if there is even a tiny feeling of heat, tension, or nausea. No matter how small the felt sensation might be, notice it. Welcome it and inwardly say hello to it.

Be curious about what emotions are present. Name them as they come into your awareness and notice where each one might be sitting in your body.

Do this for around three minutes; then become aware of your whole body. Wiggle your fingers and toes. You might like to tap your feet lightly on the floor as you gently open your eyes, look over your shoulder, notice the space you are in, and then look over the other shoulder as you fully arrive back.

You might like to take some time to journal your experience of this exercise.

Your Hero's Journey

In this chapter, you learned about the anxious adaptation, how it was created, and what it feels like as an adult. You had a peek into what it is like for those who are securely attached as adults and the benefits that come with a more secure attachment style. You have started your own hero's journey, you have taken the time to remember and linger in a secure experience, and you have experimented with being more present and grounded and have begun to develop the observer self. You have already begun the embodied practices that compound to pull you into greater internal secure attachment.

The next step in this process of building internal secure attachment is to reconnect with the wisdom of your body. In the next chapter, you will discover a powerful way of communicating with your body so it can become your safe haven, a place where you can reside, be nurtured, and find embodied safety. This body-wisdom brings with it more self-trust and self-worth, which translates into greater calm, clarity, and inner security.

CHAPTER 2

Find a Safe Haven in Your Body

Have you ever felt like your body is an uncomfortable place to be? When you're in an argument with someone you love, suddenly you are flooded with a wave of emotions. The thoughts and the sensations in your body are totally disorienting and make it difficult to think straight, much less hear what your partner is saying. The panic running through your body can feel unbearable. At times like this, your body can feel like an unsafe place. If this sounds familiar, you are not alone. With your anxious adaptation, this is a common experience when the connection in your relationship is threatened.

This happens because you didn't experience enough co-regulation as a child. When parents provide a calm approach to challenges or conflict, they help their child navigate the moment with a relaxed nervous system. The calm nervous system of the parent acts as an anchor to help the child's distressed system to return to a state of calm. When there is little co-regulation available, it is difficult to stay in your body; to separate different feelings, thoughts, and sensations; and to remain present in the conversation. As children, when we are constantly anxious about our needs being met or we are raised by someone who is overly anxious, we internalize this state of anxiety. There is no safe place internally or externally. We are unable to find a *safe haven* inside ourselves. This chapter will give you the tools to start to shift this.

Exploring Your Current Connection to Your Body

The connection to your body exists on a spectrum. You will likely feel more connected to your body at different times. It also varies from person to person. This quiz will help you assess how connected to your body you are.

Using your journal, work through the statements below and rate them according to the following scale:

True: 3 points

Sometimes true: 2 points

Not at all true: 1 point

1. I know how much sleep I need to feel my best.

2. I know what foods don't suit my body.

3. I function best if I go to bed at a particular time.

4. I can tell the difference between hunger and tiredness in my body.

5. I notice tension in my body throughout the day, and I notice where the tension is in my body.

6. I am aware and accepting of my body's natural processes, like excretion, sweating, and menstruation.

7. I am aware of hormonal shifts.

8. I am happy with my weight.

9. I notice when my breathing speeds up for any reason.

10. I can stay in contact with my body in stressful situations.

11. I never ignore my body and just keep going.

12. My body feels like a safe place for me.

13. When I feel sensations in my body, I am curious.

14. I know when I need to see a doctor or dentist and don't wait too long.

15. My body seems to support me; we are a team.

Notice if you have a lot of 1, 2, or 3s. If you seem to have a lot of 1s, be gentle. Many of us are living in cultures where we are taught to override our body in favor of productivity, acceptance, and meeting social norms. This is the beginning of a wonderful reconnection. If you have a lot of 2s, you have a more established connection to your body, which could be enhanced using the exercises in this chapter. A lot of 3s shows a deep connection and awareness of your body, that you are used to listening to its subtle messages.

Reconnecting to the Body

For the anxiously attached, it can be difficult to sense what you feel when triggered because there is so much activation. It feels like you are completely flooded with so many feelings that it is difficult to identify any individual feelings or signals coming from the body. The result is usually an explosion of deep emotion and distress and often a sense that your body is letting you down.

With practice, your body will be able to hold more sensations without reaching out to be soothed by another person or a substance, like sugar or alcohol. You will be able to make sense of the subtle differences in sensation and emotion. You will be able to hold and contain your strong feelings and bodily sensations. This is the essence of your body as a "safe haven." Your body becomes a safe and nourishing place to be, there is a sense of trust in the body, and when the body sends signals of pain or distress, you pause, listen, and attend to them. Over time, the body returns to its natural state as an intuitive extension of your soul, a safe haven.

Everything in this chapter is crafted to help you form a new safe haven in your body, develop a greater sense of self, and reconnect to your intuitive wisdom, essentially creating a secure attachment with the one person in the world who can never leave you—you!

This process of reconnection begins simply by learning to slow down and turn your attention inward. When you pause and focus inside your body, you open the doorway to a deeper connection to your authentic self, inner needs, and wisdom. Slowing down may be a welcome relief. Or it may cause discomfort. Maybe you have tried meditation, yoga, and other mindfulness practices and found them uncomfortable. If this is the case, I invite you to notice how your body responds to the idea of slowing down. As soon as you notice something, you are somehow more than the feeling; there is a sense of an "I" witnessing the feeling, the *observer self*. This process is about taking tolerable steps forward, only doing what feels right for you, but getting far enough out of your comfort zone that you can have new experiences in order for lasting change to be made.

Part of reconnecting with your body is learning to be with comfortable and uncomfortable sensations in your body. Often, we have developed an aversion to what is "uncomfortable." It might be the feeling of fire in the chest and a desire to hit out with the hands, which could be the felt experience of rage, or a wave of nausea that rises up the torso when you feel shame. Often, we have a distraction technique to avoid these sensations. The distraction might be busyness, shopping, scrolling social media, eating to push the feelings down, shopping, drinking too much alcohol, sex, or drugs. As you befriend the sensations in your body, you increase your resilience—the ability to hold a range of sensations and feelings, even contradictory ones, and reduce the need for the distractions.

Sensing Openness and Constriction in Your Body

In this exercise, you will meet the body when you are in a calm state and practice experiencing sensations of both openness and constriction to build your capacity to have awareness while experiencing a range of feelings and sensations. You will practice sensing into your body with gentleness and curiosity as you simply notice and accept everything you discover in the process without judgment.

It is best to do this exercise when you won't be disturbed, somewhere that you feel safe. It will take around ten minutes. An audio recording of this practice is available online at http://www.psycho therapycentral.health/anxious-attachment.

When you feel ready, gently turn your awareness to your body and close your eyes or lower your gaze. Notice the feeling of your body being in contact with the surface it is on. Maybe allow a sense of yourself being supported by the earth.

Next, focus on your breath and follow your breath into your body.

Start to become aware of a place in your body where you feel an openness or a softening. Notice precisely how it feels. Does it have a color? How much space does it take up? Take your time to get to know this sensation.

Next, turn your curiosity to a part of your body holding tension or constriction. Does it have a color? How much space does it take up? Take your time to get to know this sensation. There's no need to change anything; just notice and accept what is. Notice any images or emotions that come as you rest your consciousness there.

Expand your awareness now to become aware of both the area of openness and the area of constriction. Can you allow for them to both exist at the same time within you? Know that they are both parts of your current embodied experience as a human being. There is no need to change anything, just notice and allow what is.

Gently thank your body for this experience. Gently open your eyes and look around your room, over one shoulder and then the other, letting your eyes wander around your environment, bringing yourself back into your space.

Take a moment to congratulate yourself. Then get out your journal and reflect on the following questions.

- What was your experience of noticing the points where your body makes contact with the earth?

- How did it feel to accept all sensations with nonjudgment and curiosity?

- Where could you feel openness and softness?

- Where could you feel constriction?

- What was your experience of holding *both* spacious and constricted locations in your body?

This exercise helps you learn how to listen to your body, to start to identify different sensations. The body is always sending us signals, many of which we miss because we are too busy or distracted. We have forgotten how to listen. Learning to listen to the body and to be with contradiction in the body, the openness and constriction, builds resilience. With time, we become more attuned to the messages coming from the body, so they are less overwhelming. You can do this practice as often as you like, I recommend that you do it daily this week to ground this new practice in your body. You will build on this practice in the "Somatic Healing: The Six-Stage Focusing Practice" later in this chapter.

Where's Your Boundary?

Over the years of working with many people with the anxious adaptation, I have noticed a particularly weak sense of boundary. A boundary is the sense of where you end and another person starts. Boundaries help you know who is feeling what emotions. In relationship, they help others know how to treat you and are protective. They help you to say no when your inner world is clearly signaling no to you. An example of a weak boundary is accepting physical touch that doesn't feel comfortable for you. A strong boundary sounds like, "I enjoy being touched here, but not there."

If you grew up with people who lacked boundaries, you might have experienced things like unwanted touch, people going through your private things, others invading your personal space, or a lack of personal space. Boundaries become blurred when a parent becomes reliant on you or when the parents are over-involved in your life. The result is a weak sense of self because you are used to putting the needs of others first. You might feel compelled to solve all the family drama, to please everyone, feel guilty about having needs, or wanting space and find it difficult to say no.

For example, Emma is a primary school teacher in her midthirties. Emma's father died in a work accident when she was four. Her mother went through a period of intense depression and was suicidal at times. As a result of this unprocessed trauma, Emma's mother felt that the world was unsafe and grew terrified of losing Emma. She wouldn't allow Emma to do anything potentially dangerous—to swim in the ocean or ride a bike. Emma learned that the world was unsafe and she was incapable. By age ten, she was aware that she felt anxious and was especially motivated to stop her mother from being scared and reacting. So, she became skilled at monitoring her mother's mood and then moderating her behavior to keep her calm.

As an adult, Emma found it difficult to self-regulate and almost impossible to put boundaries in place. She found it challenging to sense her "self" as independent from the people she was dating. When Emma started exploring her boundary in therapy, she was shocked to realize she had no sense of a boundary. There was the tiniest sense of self hidden in the core of her body, but nothing protecting or containing that self that felt anything like a boundary.

Take a moment to think about where your boundary is. Is it your skin? Is it farther out from your skin? Or is there no sense of boundary at all? However you answered this question, know that we are all different and have a unique experience of our boundary. Contacting your physical body is especially useful in increasing your sense of embodiment and personal power.

Finding Your Edge and Exploring Touch

This exercise helps you establish a sense of your physical boundary, the skin, and the outer edge of your body. It allows you to sense yourself taking up space in the air around you and belonging in your body. This is vital when you have experienced a lack of boundaries or when your boundaries have consistently been broken as a child.

For this exercise, you will start with your hands. Using one hand to touch the other, explore what kind of touch that hand enjoys. Does it like to be stroked? Firmly or softly? Does it like to be squeezed? Firmly or softly? Does it like to be tickled? Does it like to be held?

Then change hands. How does this hand like to be touched? Does it like to be stroked, squeezed, tickled, or held? What pressure does it enjoy? Does this hand feel more or less sensitive than the other hand?

Repeat this process with your forearms, upper arms, chest, stomach area, hips, thighs, calves, and feet. Notice with curiosity what areas feel more or less sensitive, what areas seem to enjoy touch, any areas that don't enjoy it so much, and any areas that feel numb.

Now you will give the whole body a wake-up rub to help you get a felt sense of your body's outline. Choose a comfortable pressure for your body but firm enough to stimulate it. Most people find the pressure you would use to rub a loofah against your skin in the shower to exfoliate your skin is about the right pressure, but everyone is different. I invite you to find the right pressure for you. Begin with your arms and give them a good rub, as though you are waking them up. Notice the space that your arms take up. Then rub the hands, head, neck, torso, arms, thighs, knees, calves, ankles, feet, and toes. Notice if a part of your body would like more of this rubbing. If so, give it some more. Notice if a part dislikes the rubbing, and honor that.

Notice if you feel that you are in contact with your body differently after this exercise. In your journal, write about what you have learned about your body.

This exercise helps you reconnect with your body, helps you feel more embodied, and is the foundation for healthy boundaries, which you will explore in chapter 9.

Cultivating a Relationship with Your Body

I was first introduced to Focusing while studying energetic health in Australia in the early 2000s. Focusing as a modality was created by Eugene Gendlin in the 1960s when he did research on the effects of psychotherapy and found that clients who experienced a lasting positive change from psychotherapy could access a nonverbal, bodily feel of the issues that brought them into therapy (Gendlin 1964). He noticed them slowing down their speech and groping for the right words to describe feelings. For example, "Um…it's like irritation, but not quite…more like indignance. Yes! It's indignance! I feel it right here in my throat…like a fiery ball that wants to yell." This bodily-felt somatic experience is called a "felt sense" and is a powerful way to access the body's wisdom.

When I was learning about Focusing, I was still experiencing regular menstrual pain before my cycle. I thought I would see if anything around my uterus would like to be attended to in a Focusing way. I sat down, brought awareness to my body, and sensed what wanted my attention.

My attention was drawn to my left ovary. In my mind's eye, it seemed to be an orange-brownish color and looked like it was throbbing a little. I sat with it to listen and get a sense of it. I got a sense that it was hurting and sad. It felt stuck and unable to move forward. I sent it a lot of compassion and understanding, and I let it know that I was there for it.

It made sense because, at that time in my life, I was in a lot of emotional pain and felt pretty stuck in it and as if I had little agency to change the things that were causing the distress. I sat with the ovary and felt its pain. I then started to move out of the practice to become aware of my whole body and have gratitude. I began to think about making dinner and then caught myself. *Can I still feel the pain? Has anything changed?* I scanned that part of my body, and the pain had completely vanished! This was a life-changing experience for me.

I suffered from severe menstrual cramps and heavy bleeding as a teenager. My parents gave me paracetamol to cope with the pain, but as soon as it wore off, the pain returned. I was finally given hormonal tablets, which seemed to stop the pain. It was beyond my comprehension that "sitting with" and talking to a part of my body could have any physical impact on my body. I wondered why nobody had taught me this before.

When your anxious attachment adaptation is activated, you are likely to be overwhelmed by feelings and felt sensations. You are struggling with something called "interoception," defined by Elizabeth Stanley (2019) in her excellent book *Widen the Window* as "the ability to recognize bodily sensations, be aware of emotional states, and regulate physiological processes to keep the mind-body system functioning" (245). In these moments, I have found the practice of Focusing to be an invaluable tool, as it increases your capacity to notice, stay with, and decipher the meaning of what you are sensing in your body. As you are more quickly able to identify and trust your own "gut feelings," you will notice the added benefit of increased intuition. The process that follows is also useful for people who:

- experience strong emotions that are difficult to handle

- feel blocked in any area of life

- are working with addiction

- want access to a deeper intuitive awareness

- would like more self-love and self-acceptance.

Somatic Healing: The Six-Stage Focusing Practice

This practice involves six steps originally offered by Eugene Gendlin (1978). Allow yourself ten minutes of quiet time to do this process with your body. I recommend that you read through the instructions first, read the examples, and then listen to the audio version so you can try it for yourself. The audio version of this practice is available at http://www.psychotherapycentral.health/anxious-attachment.

Step 1. Clearing a Space

You might start by becoming aware of your surroundings, noticing some things in the room around you, notice what you can hear, and when you feel ready, gently lower or close your eyes.

Bring your curious, nonjudgmental awareness into your body with kindness. Become aware of the sensations in your body. Notice which areas might feel heavier, lighter, warm, cool, tingly, or achy. Don't go inside it, let there be some space between you and it.

This might sound like: *As I sense into my body, I feel an ache in my neck that has been there for a few days and something heavy and dull in my stomach. I also notice a heaviness, like a pressure on my chest.*

Step 2. Felt Sense

Notice which sensation wants your attention the most right now. Don't be tempted to merge with the felt sense; maintain some distance between it and you.

This might sound like: *I ask which one wants my attention the most right now. Immediately, the ache in my neck flares up. This is where I will focus.*

Step 3. Handle (Being with the Felt Sense)

Focus deeply on the felt sense and let any images, memories, thoughts, feeling, or movements come from the felt sense. It may be "gray and grumpy" or "moving around like a bouncing ball and a bit angry." Use your curiosity and intuition to connect with it more deeply. As you do this, remember that "it" is just a part of you; it is not all of you. You are bringing your curious, loving presence to meet this part of you.

This might sound like: *As I move toward the ache in my neck, I get a sense of its tiredness and an image comes of a tired old man sitting in a rocking chair. I observe this image and stay in contact with the felt ache in my neck.*

Step 4. Resonating (Deep Listening)

Here you give the felt sense a voice and deeply listen to it with openness and curiosity. Then check back on what it said to ensure you have got the essence of its message. Often this part of you has been holding a lot of energy, and this is its opportunity to be heard. We take time in this phase for it to express itself. There may be long silences, which is fine and allows the natural process of listening to occur.

This might sound like: *I wonder what my felt sense might like to say to me. Nothing comes. Then suddenly, the old man in his chair scowls at me and says, "You are doing too much; it's no good." I make space for what he said.*

"Yes, this part of me feels I am doing too much. Is that right?"

"Yes," he says. "You need to slow down."

I sit with what he is saying.

This step is about being with and not expecting any change. You are practicing being with whatever arises in the felt sense with curiosity and kindness.

Step 5. Asking (What Is In This Felt Sense? What Does It need?)

Take a moment to ask, "What is in this felt sense?" This is a deepening question. You have the opportunity to focus on the felt sense again and see what comes next. Take time to sense it freshly. Ask, "What does it need?" It might need a hug, more time with friends, or time alone. Take a moment to get a sense of precisely what it needs, let it know you hear it, and if it feels right for the rest of you, you might plan to meet that need.

This might sound like: *As the old man says I need to slow down, I feel a wave of tiredness come over me. I yawn. I realize I have been wanting to give up one of my commitments. I realize this is the message I have been waiting for. I naturally give a big sigh with this realization. Something shifts.*

Next, I ask the felt sense, "Is there anything you need?"

"Yes, I need you to give up that commitment; it is too much for me right now. I'm tired," it replies.

"Yes, I hear you are tired, and I'm ready to give up that commitment. How would that feel?" I ask.

"Ah, that would be amazing" (big exhale, shoulders drop as I move in my seat). "Thank you," it says.

Step 6. Receiving

Receive what came from the felt sense in a warm way. Send gratitude to the felt sense and your whole body and reorient to your space. You might like to slowly look to your left and right and gently notice a few things in your room and the sensation of your feet on the floor as you fully return.

This might sound like: *Saying "thank you" to the felt sense for all it has shared.*

Take some time to journal your experience with this practice.

Focusing is the foundation for many popular and effective somatic psychotherapy modalities today. It has stood the test of time, and I have seen it effectively change people's lives for the better in my practice and for myself. Here are some of the skills Focusing can help you develop:

- the ability to listen to your body as a form of deep intuition

- emotional intelligence

- a deeper understanding of your feelings

- an integrated emotional and physical body

- the ability to feel more at home in your body

- a stronger sense of self

- better boundaries.

I recommend that you make the "Six-Stage Focusing Practice" part of your daily routine for the next four weeks to embed the practice in your mind and body. Doing this will lead to a permanent change in how you are able to relate to your inner world and core needs.

There are other powerful body-based practices that can help you connect to the body as a safe haven. These include yoga, tai chi, and other martial arts, meditation, and massage. You might like to explore some of these as adjuncts to your work with this book.

I recommend you spend time with the exercises in this chapter and repeat them over the next few weeks. Remember that you are building a new relationship with your body. You are getting to know your body in a new way, which takes time and attention. Rather than trying to rush through this book, I invite you to drink it in slowly. Slow down and allow time and space for your healing. You deserve this.

A Secure Foundation

In this chapter, you have explored the current connection to your body and begun deepening that connection by exploring what is present, both comfortable and uncomfortable. For the body to feel safe, you need to be in contact with its edge to have a sense of where your boundary is; you strengthened this in the "Finding Your Edge and Exploring Touch" exercise. You have also learned a powerful six-step practice of listening to your body to discover your conscious and unconscious needs and wants and to be with and process what arises emotionally. Using the skills you learned in this chapter, you have the foundation for your body being your safe haven, bringing with it more self-trust and self-worth, which translates into greater calm, clarity, and inner security.

From this foundation of increased connection and embodied safety with your body, you will focus on the power of the mind and your ability to re-script your future, create new neural pathways, and break repeating cycles in your life.

CHAPTER 3

Your Mind Can Script Your Future

Each thought alters the physical state of your brain synapses at a microscopic level.

—Norman Doidge, *The Brain that Changes Itself*

Jasmin walked into my office looking frazzled. She said, "I'm going completely crazy. I've just spent the hour bus ride here stalking Manjit's ex-girlfriend on the internet, looking at who she's friends with, and where she's been on vacation. I couldn't stop myself. Deep down, I know she's better than me, which is ridiculous because I've never met her, and Manjit dumped her. This morning he mentioned that she had worked at the same place as our friend, and they knew each other. That was all he said. But I felt this alarm go off. I wondered if he had been thinking about or in contact with her. Then I wondered if they were still friends on social media. Then I had to know…I just couldn't stop my mind; it was out of control with anxiety and panic."

This is a common scenario when you have an anxious adaptation and your attachment system gets activated. You feel that the relationship is somehow threatened, real, or imagined. Part of healing the anxious adaptation is learning to work on the mind and change old scripts of fear and self-judgment. A script is a deeply embedded series of beliefs and expectations about yourself, others, and the world around you. The more you are the master of your mind, the less anxious you feel and the more stable you are for yourself as a safe haven.

Neuroplasticity

The brain is perhaps one of the body's most explored yet least understood organs. What we do now know about the brain is that it grows and changes throughout your lifetime and *rewires* with every experience, meaning new neural networks are created as you develop new skills or have new experiences. When you do something repeatedly, you increase the myelin (a fatty coating around the nerves) on those nerve pathways, allowing the signals to move faster. This increases your tendency to do that thing automatically. Just think about learning to drive. After a year or so of regular driving, much of it is automatic because you have built new thickly myelinated neural networks.

Unless you consciously create new networks, you will use the old ones. You might have an old script that says, *When I'm sad, buy something, and I'll feel better*, and every time you do this, you strengthen that script, making it more likely that the next time you feel sad, you will buy something. You do this compulsively because that is how your brain is wired until you try to create a new script. This is why breaking old habits and creating new ones is difficult. You must go against your old programming while building a new neural network to support the new practice.

As part of a research study, a group of healthy individuals participated in an eight-week mindfulness-based stress-reduction course where participants learned various meditation techniques (Hölzel et al. 2010). Participants' rated their stress levels before and after the study and magnetic resonance imaging (MRI) images were taken of their brains. Participants reported significantly reduced stress, and researchers found a corresponding reduction of gray matter in the basolateral amygdala, which is part of the limbic system (emotional system) and important in stress responses, showing that *as our psychological state changes, so too does our brain.*

The good news about neuroplasticity is that we can influence our brain patterning. Neuroplastic change requires us to first "notice" our natural response, something you practiced in the "Noticing" exercise in chapter 1. This gives us a natural pause as we enter the observer state and delays our automatic reaction. Then we can put our attention somewhere safer consciously.

How Your Thoughts and Beliefs Influence Your Lived Experience

Look at this picture of a cat and notice what you feel in your body and your thoughts. What would you like to do if you were to interact with it?

Now, imagine that you had been bitten or scratched by a cat, notice what you feel in your body, what thoughts you have, and if you still want to interact with it.

This is how our thoughts and past experiences affect our *felt* experiences and our behavior.

What Are Your Core Beliefs?

A core belief is deeply held and known to be true to you. Your core beliefs can usually be traced back to childhood experiences and events. Still, they continue to be reinforced by present-day circumstances.

Discovering Your Negative Core Conscious Beliefs

Our core beliefs have often come from our family of origin and the culture in which we were raised.

To gain a deeper understanding of your family and their beliefs, I invite you to do some journaling and answer the questions below.

Family of origin:

- Where did your family come from?

- Who were the members of your core family?

- Did your family experience trauma, like abuse, war, immigration, or mental health issues?

- What do you imagine that was like for them?

- How do you think those experiences impacted your parents' parenting style?

- What core beliefs about relationships and the world did your parents have?

Your childhood:

- Were your needs for love, acceptance, nourishment, encouragement, and safety met?

- If not, why not?

- How were you disciplined?

- How did your parents' (or caregivers') parenting style impact you?

- Were there any major disruptions, like the loss of a family member, suicide, extended time away from your parents, financial issues, affairs, or divorce?

- What impact did these events have on you and your family?

- Looking back, what strengths or skills do you feel you developed because of your experiences?

- What core beliefs might have emerged from these experiences?

Your Negative Core Beliefs

What are your core beliefs about yourself? For example: *I'm flawed, difficult to love, and too reactive.*

What are your beliefs about others? For example: *Other people are better than me, people leave me, and others can't be trusted.*

What are your beliefs about the world? For example: *The world is unsafe, the world is unreliable, and I need to be in a relationship to be safe.*

Well done for taking an honest inventory of your conscious negative beliefs. As you read your responses, please remember that these beliefs came from somewhere and that all beliefs can be changed with love, patience, and commitment.

Now let's look at some unconscious beliefs.

Discovering Your Unconscious Beliefs

An unconscious belief is something we know to be true but are not consciously aware of. It is usually something that was true during childhood and now runs on autopilot as a given truth. Here you will use chapter 2's "Somatic Healing: The Six-Stage Focusing Practice" to explore your unconscious beliefs. An audio recording of this practice is available online at http://www.psychotherapycentral.health/anxious-attachment.

Allow ten minutes of quiet time and find a safe and relaxing space for you to focus and tune in to your body in this mindful way.

Take a moment to notice your surroundings, and gently close or lower your eyes when you feel ready. Take a deep breath with a long exhale and then turn your awareness inward with curiosity and compassion.

Step 1. Awareness. Notice in your body any areas of discomfort or pain and gently take your attention there. Notice which area would most like your attention right now and gently focus there with kindness and curiosity, like moving to sit next to an old friend.

Step 2. Connection. Take a moment to get a sense of "it." Notice if it shows up as an image, word, phrase, or feeling. Just notice what comes without any judgment.

Step 3. Deep listening. When the time feels right, ask what beliefs it is holding. Listen carefully for an answer and go with the first thing that pops into your mind. Once you have it, check if this part has any other beliefs about you, others, or the world it would like to add? Let it know that you are listening and present.

Step 4. Gratitude. When it feels complete, thank the felt sense and your whole body, and slowly reorientate to your space. You might like to slowly look to your left and right and notice a few things in your room and the sensation of your feet on the floor as you fully return.

Now that you have completed these exercises, you have a list of conscious and unconscious beliefs to work with in the rest of this chapter.

Exploring More Supportive Beliefs with the Body

Now you have uncovered some core beliefs, let's explore their impact and find some alternatives. Choose one of your beliefs from the "Discovering Your Negative Core *Conscious* Beliefs" exercise. We are going to take a moment to explore this more fully. Following are some instructions on actions to take with your body. This may feel strange or embarrassing at first. Find a safe, quiet place where you can be yourself and commit to the process. Be gentle with yourself, leaving all judgment aside, be supportive of yourself in this process, and allow yourself to relax into it. If you "play this game," you will begin to experience the benefits.

The Unsupportive Belief

Posture. Stand up and allow your body to move into the posture that best represents your chosen belief. Take a moment to connect with the statement deeply and then exaggerate the associated posture to help you experience it more fully.

Explore. From this posture, what does life feel like? What emotions come naturally from this posture? What does it feel like the future holds?

Sara chose the belief "I'm always abandoned" and found that her upper spine fell forward, her shoulders collapsed to the sides, and she felt constricted in her chest. It was difficult to breathe, and her head went down, so she was looking at the floor. Her arms felt numb and limp. There was no energy in her body.

Exploring a More Supportive Belief

Choose a belief that you think is more supportive than your original belief.

Sara chose "I am kind and worthy of intimate relationships."

Posture. Move into the stance that best represents your supportive belief. Imagine that it is absolutely accurate and describes your life and experience exactly.

Notice what happens to your spine, torso, legs, arms, neck, and head. Where do your eyes want to look?

When Sara did this, she immediately grew about four inches as she straightened her spine and moved her shoulders back and her head lifted. She took a deep breath and said, "Wow. That feels SO much better." She noticed that her chin felt higher than usual, and her shoulders were farther back. She smiled and said she felt a burst of energy in her upper chest. She noticed her legs felt energized, like they were about to dance or play with someone. She felt joy in her body!

Explore. From this posture, what does life feel like? What emotions come naturally from this posture? What other thoughts emerge? What does the future feel like it holds?

Challenge. Challenge yourself to hold this new belief and pose twice a day. They might be subtle changes, but they can be powerful. Spend a few minutes standing in your new posture, exploring the new thoughts, emotions, and ways of being in the world that emerge. As you do this, you are creating new neural pathways, imprinting a new body memory and new possibilities for your life.

Exploring Your Beliefs

Now you're going to capture your experience in table form so you have a concise summary of how your beliefs affect you. Record your experience in the right column. Copy the following table or download a blank version online at http://www.psychotherapycentral.health/anxious-attachment.

Unsupportive belief: e.g., *I'm always abandoned.*	
Posture: e.g., *Spine leaning forward, head hanging down, shoulders slumped, no energy.*	
Explore: What does life feel like from here?	
Explore: What emotions emerge?	
Explore: What does the future hold?	
More supportive belief: e.g., *I am kind and worthy of intimate relationships.*	
Posture: e.g., *Spine straight, head is upright, and my eyes are staring straight ahead. I am smiling.*	
Explore: What does life feel like from here?	
Explore: What emotions emerge?	
Explore: What does the future hold?	

Secure Base Scripts

Research into the scripts used by securely attached people gives us insight into the working of their minds. These are useful to explore so you can start to create neural networks of security for yourself.

Common scripts for the securely attached include (Waters and Waters 2006; Mikulincer, et al. 2009):

- If I am distressed, I can reach out to someone I know for help.

- When I reach out, they will be available and able to assist.

- I will experience relief and comfort by being close to this person.

I suggest you work with these scripts as you did in the exercise above. For example, you might choose to work with *When I reach out, others are unavailable* as your "unsupportive belief." Perhaps, *When I reach out, people are available and able to assist* is your "more supportive belief."

Finding the Antidote Experiences and Memories—Real or Imagined

When we have experienced a difficult childhood, there is a tendency to focus the spotlight of the mind on the things that were harmful. A powerful part of working with our mind is to practice having the spotlight of the mind focused on positive experiences, what I like to call "antidote" memories, to build new neural networks of positivity. For example, you might have an expectation in your relationship that you will be cheated on (part of an abandonment script). Maybe your father cheated on your mother repeatedly, and every partner you have had has cheated on you, so you expect your current partner will eventually cheat on you. Then you start to challenge that script. Are there any times someone has been faithful to you? Maybe you remember your best friend keeping a secret you told them. This is a kind of faithfulness. You linger here. What does it feel like to know they kept your secret? Then you think about past partners, and you remember someone you dated for a few months in high school and that they were faithful to you. You linger here, and you turn the spotlight on that memory. What does it feel like to remember that they were trustworthy? In this way, you start to harness the power of the mind, and rather than being a victim of your unruly monkey mind, you become the master.

Many clients find it helpful to have a specific go-to memory to counter a particular script. You might explore a few antidote memories and then use the one with the most positive emotional charge. If you struggle to find anything as an antidote to a specific script, imagine what it would feel like to experience the remedy. For example, what would it feel like if you were in a committed relationship with a trustworthy person? What would it feel like to live with this person, to come home to them? How does your body feel around them? What thoughts do you have about the person? How does your posture change as you imagine this reality? If you have no lived experience of faithfulness, you might find it helpful to find a healthy template from a TV show or movie. Choose a character portrayed as faithful to their partner, who is kind and supportive, and then imagine being their partner. This is not to create a fantasy about a TV star but to fill in a missing experience. If you have no experience of faithfulness in your life, this can be considered a missing experience. With neuroplasticity, you can start to fill in that gap.

Utilizing Your Antidote Experiences to Change Your Mind

In this exercise, you will learn how to identify a target belief and antidote experience to build a positive neural network.

Step 1. Identify a target belief. Choose one of your beliefs from the "Discovering Your Negative Core *Conscious* Beliefs" exercise above to work with. Let's choose *I'm difficult to love* for a demonstration.

Step 2. Identify antidote memories. Challenge yourself to think of as many instances as you can of when you felt loved, for example:

- I felt loved by my grandfather. He was always happy to see me and bought me gifts.

- My dog, Oli, is always happy to see me. I feel love from her.

- My high school friend Melissa cared for me. When our peers pushed me around, she stuck up for me a few times.

Step 3. Build new networks. Choose the most potent experience to help you build new networks. Linger in your chosen memory for sixty seconds or more, remembering the event's details and embellishing it with extra richness. For example, remember how it felt in your grandfather's embrace. How tight was it? What did he smell like? What are you both wearing? What feelings do you feel in your body as you relive that hug?

Imprint the memory of that experience. Invite your body and mind to remember what this feels like from the inside.

Step 4. Focus on moving forward. If you were to carry this new belief into your life:

- What might your life look like?

- How might you be different with this new attitude?

- What different things might happen in your life?

A Word About Grief

On this healing journey, you will most likely encounter pockets of unexpressed grief. The grief of what was experienced and what was missing. In my experience, people tend to give themselves more permission to grieve what happened to them than to mourn what they missed out on. Permit yourself to grieve the absence of love, acceptance, protection, and encouragement.

This grief might come up unexpectedly. As it does, allow it, *notice* it. Notice what thoughts, emotions, and sensations accompany it. Be curious about it and remember that crying is a natural response to many situations. It often relieves stress. When we cry, oxytocin and endorphins (the happy chemicals that ease physical and emotional pain) are released and sleep is improved. I wonder how it would be if we shifted the relationship with our tears. If, instead of pushing them back, we allowed them? Nobody has ever not stopped crying—eventually. I often think of tears as a release of pent-up energy, an expression of something held deep within coming to the surface. Tears make us more human and more vulnerable. We can connect through tears.

Cocreating with Your Mind

In this chapter, you explored some of the conscious and unconscious beliefs that keep you stuck in repeated cycles of behavior and prevent you from moving toward a more secure attachment style. You explored what supportive beliefs feel like in your body and emotionally. You have spent time finding powerful "antidote" memories to help build new neural pathways of more connected, secure experiences. The key to this chapter is to remember the plastic nature of the brain and your ability to change your long-held, repetitive thoughts, beliefs, and behaviors. This is not a chapter that you do once and forget about, these exercises need to be done repeatedly to be effective. "The brain changes slowly, in increments. The same circuits have to fire repeatedly to create a reliable new neural pathway that will lead to a different reaction" as psychologists Pat Ogden and Janina Fisher explain (2015, 163). You might set aside some time every day to spend time consciously changing your mind. In the next chapter, you will begin the vital work of learning to care for your younger self to form a secure attachment with the most important person in your life: you!

CHAPTER 4

Heal Emotionally with a New Parenting Experience

Have you ever been in a situation where you are triggered and find yourself behaving like a six-year-old? You know you are not being rational, but you cannot stop yourself from reacting in the way you are. This is your inner child taking over and dealing with the situation as a child would, from a child's perspective, with the tools and wisdom available to a child. The inner child is part of you that remembers everything that happened in your childhood and is still looking for the co-regulation that was inconsistent or nonexistent from your caregivers. The good news is that as an adult, you can now give this love, attunement, and care to your inner child and effectively heal some aspects of the original attachment wound. In the process, you will learn how to shift critical self-talk and amplify your loving inner voice. This work is life-changing for your anxious adaptation because you are forming a secure inner attachment between your wounded child parts and your nurturing inner parent.

Inner Child and Reparenting

Inner child work grew out of Eric Berne's (1964) transactional analysis, and different forms of this work have been incorporated into many evidence-based strands of psychotherapy since then. I have been doing inner child work on myself and with my clients since my twenties. It is one of the most effective ways to improve self-regulation, change your critical internal dialogue, cultivate more self-acceptance, and improve your relationships.

The best part about doing this work is that you learn to be with and attend to the scared and vulnerable part of yourself—and simultaneously grow the loving, compassionate parent part. Your fear of abandonment dissipates because of a deep connection with self and the promise that you will never leave your inner child. It is no longer possible for you to be abandoned by your partner *and* yourself. You stand firm as an ever-present loving parent to your inner child. You begin to imprint in the psyche the felt sense of having a consistent, attuned presence. This is how inner child work helps heal anxious attachment to have more fulfilling, intimate, healthy relationships.

Learning to reparent yourself is a commitment. You need to build trust with your inner child, be reliable, and take care of them. When you learn to reparent, you have the opportunity to learn how to:

- tune in to your authentic needs at any moment

- validate your reality

- be kind to yourself rather than critical

- say no when you need to

- put healthy boundaries in place

- comfort yourself when you are feeling a strong emotion.

What Is the Inner Child?

The best way to think about the inner child is as part of your psyche that remembers your childhood experiences and is still impacted by many of them. Like most toddlers, the inner child feels emotions and lets them flow through, and is naturally creative, spontaneous, curious, and joyful. You may have experienced a childhood that was less than optimal. Maybe the playful, exuberant child you were wasn't safe to be seen. Perhaps you were neglected or shamed. For many reasons, as we grow, we tend to hide the vulnerable parts of ourselves and lose our natural joy and spontaneity, perhaps experiencing anxiety and depression as a result. We are all in a relationship with our inner child. For most people, it is an unconscious relationship. With this book, you can change this and make it *conscious*.

Inner child work is the process of reconnecting with and healing the parts of you that were hurt during your childhood. You can reach back through time, hold your child's hand, and give them the support they need to help integrate their experiences.

The inner child doesn't have a set age because this part of your psyche acts as a gateway into unprocessed childhood experiences that might have happened at any age. For this reason, you can think of your inner child as the gateway to your younger parts.

Discovering the Nurturing Inner Parent

One of the most exciting aspects of inner child work is the discovery and amplification of your *nurturing* inner parent. This is the part of you that might come forward when you see an injured animal or a lost child. It is the part that wants to step forward with a gentle voice, soft eyes, and a big heart. It wants to reach out tenderly and provide love and protection.

Many of us are familiar with another type of inner parent, the *critical* inner parent. This part of you often sounds judgmental, has a harsh voice when you make mistakes, and struggles to find compassion or softness when you most need it. For example, after threatening to break up with your partner, this inner voice might say, "Well, now you've done it. This one is over too. You'll be alone forever because there's something wrong with you." Sometimes you'll find these scripts are different versions of what was said in your childhood. They have become internalized, or the words are different, but the flavor of what is being shared is similar. When you do inner child work, you are choosing to amplify the voice of the *nurturing* inner parent and create more robust neural pathways of self-love and acceptance.

The nurturing parent feels similar to your Higher Self or soul. It is unconditionally loving and attentive; has loving boundaries; is kind, creative, courageous, and curious; and speaks with a soothing, gentle tone.

The nurturing parent likes to hug your child and is playful and allowing. When you bring forth the part of you that is the inner parent, you have the opportunity to tell your inner child the things they deserved to hear as children but may not have heard. It can be powerful for your child to hear something like: "You are so beautiful on the inside and the outside. You are the most important person in my life. I *love* being with you and playing with you. I love you if you misbehave. I love you if you are well-behaved. I love you no matter what."

Many of us have never experienced unconditional love, but you can change that! Learning to give yourself the unconditional love you needed but didn't receive as a child is life-changing. It transforms the deep feelings of disconnect, inadequacy, and critically focusing on your flaws into unconditional self-acceptance, self-compassion, and love. You begin to reconnect with your authentic needs and take care of yourself in a new way with improved boundaries and a much stronger sense of self. This is the process of creating inner secure attachment.

The Nurturing Parent Role Model

Unfortunately, in my clinic, I meet many people who lack the inner experience of what a nurturing parent might feel, sound, and look like in action. Many people have shared how helpful it has been to have a role model or archetypal character to hold in mind as they form their nurturing parent voice. This helps them think of the words and tone that person would use to speak to their inner child. Some characters you might like to use for the inner mother might be Mary Poppins, Mother Mary, or the Hindu goddess Durga—a woman with kindness, acceptance, and the power to keep you safe and put healthy boundaries in place. For the inner father, you might like to use Jesus, the Hindu god Brahma, or Frank Dunphy from *Modern Family*. Again, you are looking for someone who is kind, loving, and protective as an inner father. You might find that you have healthy role models in your family or at work.

Reparenting: A Form of Deep Inner Healing

Reparenting is the opportunity for a new relational experience. Rather than your younger self being met with frustration, criticism, or neglect, you have the chance to learn what your inner child needs and to meet those needs with a sense of love and attunement that was absent in your childhood. This is a form of deep inner healing.

Wherever you are in your healing journey, reparenting is part of it. When you have been raised by adults who didn't know how to regulate their nervous systems and couldn't model healthy boundaries or conflict resolution due to their upbringing, you need to learn these skills later in life as an adult. Your parents simply couldn't teach you what they didn't know or couldn't do for themselves or you.

It is possible to learn to reparent yourself, to learn how to be present with the scared and lonely inner child who feels not good enough, rejected, and hurt. As you reparent, you learn to sit with the inner child in painful moments and to acknowledge and validate the pain. You learn to speak to yourself in the form of the inner child with the greatest love and compassion.

Magic occurs when you pause, connect with the wounded part of self, and hold space for it. I have witnessed countless moments of deep healing occur in such moments. Working with my inner child and nurturing parent has been one of the most empowering connections I have made. I have developed a knowing that I will always be there for *me*. I don't need to outsource my need for love, acceptance, or approval because I love, accept, and approve of my inner child daily. She looks to me for reassurance in times of stress. For me, inner child healing is never finished. *It is a relationship.* It is the most important relationship I have—the one with myself.

The narratives you have lived with for so long start to change as you gain insight into the situation through your new adult lens. Know that everyone can learn reparenting skills. It might be the missing piece of the puzzle for you.

What Is It Like to Meet Your Inner Child?

People often tell me that they have read books and listened to podcasts about the inner child, but they have struggled to have a meaningful *felt* experience of the presence of their inner child. The inner child is not a mental construct to be analyzed and discussed. The inner child is the container for many of your strong emotions and unprocessed trauma; the inner child is a felt experience. When reaching out to your inner child, try not to think about it—just feel their presence.

In my work as a psychotherapist and energetic healer, about 95 percent of my clients who meet their inner child for the first time with me have an emotional, heart-warming experience. They often leave that first meeting feeling "somehow relieved," like "a big weight has been lifted from my shoulders," and often a little teary. Many people report feeling immense relief to have reconnected with their inner child and a tremendous sense of empowerment in accepting the new role as the parent of this child.

Inner Child Healing Meditation

Find a quiet place to be alone for twenty minutes. You might like to light a candle and set up something that feels like a sacred space. Find a comfortable place to sit or lie down, somewhere you can allow yourself to relax deeply. When you are ready, close your eyes, take a deep breath, and gift this time to yourself and your inner child. This is a time to remember the love that you are.

I recommend that you listen to this meditation so you can relax into it fully and be guided by my voice. An audio recording of this practice is available online at http://www.psychotherapycentral.health /anxious-attachment.

> *Take a deep breath and let go of anything distracting you, knowing you can return to it after the meditation is complete. You might notice that some parts of you feel anxious or resistant to meeting your inner child. Remind those parts that you are now an adult, give them any reassurance they might*

need, and ask them to stand to the side while you meet your child.

Bring your attention to your breath. Notice your chest moving up and down. Gently guide the breath into your belly and begin to notice the subtle sensations in your body. Breathe into any discomfort and let it go. Imagine all tension draining out of your body as you deeply relax.

You are going on a journey to meet your inner child. Know that whatever your inner child brings forward today, it is perfect. This is a safe space, and everything is welcome here. Breathe in and out of your own heart, and let it expand. You will call your inner child to be with you here.

As your inner child approaches, imagine love emanating from your heart toward them. Visualize your inner child standing before you and notice how old they are. Welcome them with a warm smile and spend a moment connecting with them through your heart, sharing how glad you are to see them.

Let them know you are sorry they were alone for so long and you are here now to love and protect them. Let them know that you are all grown-up and you will do your absolute best to be the most caring and kind parent you can be. That you love them unconditionally. This means that you love them no matter what, if they pass or fail, if they are good or bad, and that there is nothing they can do to stop you from loving them.

Remind them that as a child, it is their job to be a child, to play and have fun, and not to worry about adult things or the adults around them. It was never their job to care for adults as a child, to take care of the adults' emotions. Let them know that they are perfect and that you are glad they are your inner child.

Ask them how they are feeling and take time to listen deeply.

Validate what they share and give them permission to be angry, sad, or confused. Imagine being their best friend and being totally on their side about anything they share with you—a supportive, loving presence.

Take a moment to share anything else you would like to say, and notice if there is anything your inner child would like to hear from you.

Let your inner child respond. If they are quiet, simply be with them with all your presence, there is no hurry, no pressure. You will be back to see them regularly from now on.

Ask if they would like a hug. If they would, give them a gentle, loving hug. Feel their little heart beating and notice the smell of their hair and let them know how much you love them. Ask them how often they would like to meet and what time of day suits them best.

When you are ready, allow your heart to fill with light and imagine your inner child shrinking in size, to about two inches tall. They merge with that light and go into the light of your heart, becoming one with your heart. In your heart space, see them happy, safe, and protected.

Let any worried parts of you that stood aside to allow this meeting to happen see your inner child in your heart and thank them.

You are now reconnected to your inner child. You can care for them; you can love them. Take a deep breath and become aware of your body again. Move your hands and feet and thank yourself for this special experience. Become aware of the heart area where your inner child resides, knowing they are always there. Bring this new connection and awareness into the room as you open your eyes.

Journal Prompts

In your journal, write about this experience in as much detail as you can. Consider the following questions:

- How old was your inner child?

- How did they respond to you?

- What did they want to share with you?

- What did they most like to hear from you?

- How often would your child like to connect with you moving forward, and did they have a preference for a time of day?

Integration

When doing the above meditation for the first time, you might have a baby or teenager come forward to represent your inner child. I invite you to trust what comes. If your child appears as a baby, care for the baby as you would a real baby, talking with a soothing voice, holding them in your arms, rocking them, and maybe singing or humming to them. If your child appears as a teenager, treat them as you would a teenager you love and respect. I find that talking to them in the language you spoke at their age is also beneficial. When you listen to the meditation audio, translate it for your inner child if necessary.

When doing this meditation, you may find it is difficult to stay separate from your inner child and become merged. If this happens, return to the meditation and keep separating from your inner child so you can attend to them as your nurturing parent. Be patient with your process and keep placing the inner child outside you and growing the nurturing parent part of you that is caring for your child. With repetition, this becomes easier over time.

Your inner child may be hesitant to interact at first. You might stay at a comfortable distance to your child and let them know you are not going anywhere and that you will be there when they are ready to make more contact without pressure. By staying in contact with them and being reliable, unconditionally loving, and nonjudgmental, your inner child will learn to trust you.

Most people's inner children have been holding a vast amount of unexpressed grief, so it is common to feel a lot of sadness when you first meet your inner child. This can be confusing if you think nothing terrible happened in your childhood. You might be grieving the lack of care, attunement, and felt love from your parents, not only major traumas. Or your child might be expressing their sadness at being alone for so long. Let the grief flow through and be expressed while you hold your inner child.

During this meditation, you may have had the feeling that you are unable to care for your child in the way they need. As the nurturing parent, your promise to your inner child is that you will try your best and get the support you need to be the best possible parent. As a parent, you are not perfect, and you won't always have all the answers for your inner child. You can promise that you will always tell them the truth and do your best to take care of them.

Helping Your Inner Child Label Emotions

A ground-breaking study using functional magnetic resonance imaging data to look at the brain activity of participants confirmed that "putting feelings into words" had a direct effect on brain activity (Lieberman et al. 2007, 421). I can't count the times I have sat in a session with a client and waited with curiosity as they described an event and then tried to name the emotion. It often sounds like, "I was so angry! Um…actually, it was a bit different to angry." As they pause and check in with the feeling, I can almost hear them touching it and trying to find the most resonant word; then they come back up for breath with the hidden treasure. "I was *incensed*! That's it, *incensed*." With that, there is often a deep breath in, an exhale, and a palpable shift in the room once the feeling has been identified and given a name.

Learning to name emotions is part of our emotional development, and doing it with our inner child is part of the reparenting process. It is in slowing down, attending to the inner child, and listening with curiosity that helps them to explore and name their emotions.

When you do the inner child meditation, you may find them in an emotional state—perhaps confused, acting out, or expressing emotion through gritted teeth or tears. You can support them by asking them to put words to their feelings. Then talk to them about why they are feeling this way and offer them support and validation. Their clarity can become your clarity—which can lead to profound healing experiences.

What Does Your Child Most Want to Hear?

Your inner child wants to hear the messages they most missed out on. So, if you were repeatedly *abandoned* as a child, your inner child will need a lot of reassurance from you that you are not going anywhere and will be checking in on them regularly.

If your inner child was not adequately *protected*, they will likely want to feel your protection. That might mean feeling safe in your home environment, to know that you will stand up for them at work with your pushy colleague, or to simply hear, "I have your back. Nobody is going to hurt you again."

If you received the message as a child that you are somehow *flawed* because of your strong feelings, your inner child would like to hear, "You are a little child, so of course you have big feelings. I'm okay with your big feelings. Perhaps the adults around you didn't have the time or capacity to care for you in the way you needed. I'm so sorry about that. I'm here for you now, and I have all the time and energy in the world for you. I love you."

Every time you check in with your inner child, address their core wounds in this way. It is profoundly healing for your child to hear these messages on repeat as you create new neural pathways of love and acceptance. As you do, be sure to use language that is appropriate to the age of your inner child. If they appear as a six-year-old, use language that a six-year-old would understand. If they appear as a baby, talk to them like a real-life baby, using a gentle voice and simple language. You can do this out loud or in your head. I suggest trying both and exploring what feels best for you.

Here are some additional things your inner child might like to hear from you.

- I love you very, very much. You are completely lovable just as you are.

- I love you for who you are, not what you do.

- I love you if you are the best in the class and if you are the worst.

- It's okay to feel feelings. All feelings are welcome here.

- I forgive you for all the mistakes you have ever made. You were a child, not an adult.

- It is not your job to take care of the adults around you.

- I will take care of adult situations, like relationships and work. Your job is to have fun and play.

- Because I am over eighteen, I will be your mom and dad now. I'm going to take care of you.

- I'm going to keep you safe.

- I'm so sorry you weren't shown the love you deserved when you were a child. I want to help you feel loved by me now.

- I love spending time with you. What would you like to do with me this weekend?

Meeting the Needs of Your Inner Child

The best way to identify your inner child's needs is to do the inner child meditation and ask your inner child directly. You might be surprised by the answers you get. Once you have the request, you can move through the following three-step process of validation, negotiation, and offering.

Step 1. Validate. When we have the anxious attachment adaptation, we have often grown up with a severe lack of validation. Often our feelings and experiences have been invalidated, so our inner child is desperate for validation. Whatever your inner child shares with you, be sure to validate their experiences, thoughts, and feelings. Nothing can be wrong because it is their experience. Your job here is to be unconditionally loving and supportive. This is often something your inner child has never experienced and is profoundly healing. Take time with this step of the process. You are rewiring your brain for new, more supportive experiences in the future.

Step 2. Negotiate. Your role here is to help your inner child identify realistic and healthy needs. Sometimes the inner child will ask for a need to be met by someone else. You can't control this, so keep asking the child to identify a need that you can meet as the nurturing parent. The inner child might also ask for something that is not good for them, for example, a bottle of wine or a whole tub of ice cream. When this happens, negotiate with the child, just as you would with a real-life child. This is part of healthy parenting. It is providing the child with guidance and healthy boundaries and explaining what is good for them in a way they can understand.

Step 3. Offer. As best you can, in a selfless way, offer your inner child what they have asked for.

Here are a couple of example dialogues to get you started. Hopefully they will help you find your nurturing inner parenting voice.

Your inner child says: *"I need attention."*

Step 1. Validate.

Nurturing parent: *Yes, of course you need attention. That is so natural; you are a child and deserve attention and adoration. I wonder what I could do to help you feel you are getting the attention you deserve?*

Inner child: *I need Tom to be giving me more attention than he is. I'm not sure if he loves me.*

Nurturing parent: *Yes, I feel that too.*

Step 2. Negotiate.

Nurturing parent: *I can't control what Tom does or how he's feeling but know that I am right here for you and that I love you very much. I wonder what I could do to help you feel you are getting the attention you deserve?*

Inner child: *First, I would like a hug, and then I would like you to tell me that everything is going to be okay. I feel scared.*

Step 3. Offer.

Nurturing parent: *I understand why you feel scared. That makes sense; falling in love is vulnerable and scary. Know that I'm here with you through this and that I am never going anywhere.*

You give your inner child the hug they asked for, lingering in this hug. You make sure they know you can stay here for as long as they need. They have your full attention.

> *Everything is going to be okay because I am never going to leave you. I don't know what will happen with Tom, but know I will be here to keep you safe and deal with Tom because I am the parent. Your job is to play and have fun; I'll take care of the relationship with Tom.*

When your inner child hears this, they often release a natural deep sigh, feeling reassured and calm.

Your inner child says: *"I need ice cream."*

Step 1. Validate.

Nurturing parent: *I hear you. I know you are feeling some strong feelings right now and want to eat a tub of ice cream. You hope feeling full of ice cream might make you feel better. I get that.*

Step 2. Negotiate.

Nurturing parent: *Eating the whole tub of ice cream is not going to make those feelings go away, and remember how last time we did that, we ended up in a pit of shame? I am here for you. What else might you need at this moment, here with me?*

Inner child: *I feel scared. I just need you to be here with me and to know you won't leave me.*

Nurturing parent: *I am right here with you. I am not going anywhere, and I am going to keep you safe. Let's sit together for as long as you like.*

Nurturing parent: *Is there anything else you need right now?*

Inner child: *I feel exhausted. Can we go to bed and read for a while with a cup of mint tea?*

Step 3. Offer.

Nurturing parent: *Yes, I would love that. I love hanging out with you.*

Exploring Your Creativity and Playfulness

Many of you had parents who were overly serious and not in touch with their inner children and did not allow you to spend time being a child. You might have been prevented from being messy, making mistakes, and being creative for fun. Perhaps you grew up with parents whose inner children were out of control, with no stability or boundaries. This can be frightening for children and cause them to grow up too quickly, feeling that they must take care of their parents. In both cases, you effectively lost out on your childhood and on being playful and spontaneous. The next exercise can help.

Rediscover Creativity and Playfulness

One of the most significant benefits of doing inner child work is connecting with the creative and playful energy that can be released back into your energetic system after being trapped for so many years. Spend some time responding to the following questions in your journal and make some time for fun and play.

Childhood

- Think back to being a child. What do you remember doing as a child that you enjoyed? It might be playing dress-up, playing with trains, playing with dolls, playing with your dog, running, skipping, doing handstands, playing hide and seek, drawing, writing, or playing let's pretend.

- If your inner child would like to do one of these activities in the next week with you, which one would they choose?

Make a promise to your child and yourself to do that thing this week.

Adulthood

- As an adult, what do you do now for fun? What makes you laugh and feel uplifted? It might be walking your dog in the park, going to dinner with friends, baking, going to concerts, playing the guitar, painting, or camping.

- If you could choose something to do next week, which would you and your inner child choose?

Find a time in the next week to do that thing.

When Your Inner Child Feels Abandoned

Jada had always struggled with feelings of abandonment after losing her mother at three years old. When her partner went away for work, she would feel distraught and want her to return, or she would keep her on the phone for hours in the evening after her conferences, and she would end up feeling exhausted.

When Jada first met her inner child, she was five years old. Her inner child was terrified of losing Jada and wanted to be in a pouch on her chest at all times. Jada let her stay there in the meditation and stressed how she loved being close to her and how she could never leave little Jada because she is part of her. Little Jada found it incredibly reassuring to know that they could never be separated, and Jada became quite emotional with this *felt sense* of always having someone there to take care of her.

Jada had decided to talk to her inner child once a day to see how she was and what she needed, and she had started to look forward to these daily check-ins. She found that her inner child had become increasingly confident when talking to her and cheeky in her requests. Little Jada was beginning to trust that nurturing parent Jada would always be there for her.

Without warning, Jada's partner was called away for an emergency at work and had to be away for two nights. Jada immediately sat down to check in with little Jada. Here is how she describes the experience.

"I couldn't believe it. Little Jada asked me what we would get up to while my partner was away. I thought about it and suggested a bath and a movie. Little Jada said it sounded too boring and that she'd prefer to hang out with our friend Laura and cook dinner. I thought that was a great idea, so we did. I even forgot that my partner was away until I drove home that night. Whenever I thought little Jada might get triggered, I checked in with her. It was like she felt my love and concern and suddenly didn't feel alone anymore. I was so proud of myself and her. It's been a huge shift for me."

Maintaining a Connection with Your Inner Child

Now you have met your inner child, it is your job to be their nurturing parent, to connect with them regularly, and to cultivate a loving, trusting relationship. Meeting them once and forgetting about them will not cultivate the relationship within that you are looking for. The inner child greatly appreciates even a short daily check-in. I like to think about little Jenny as a real child. There is no way I would go for a whole day without speaking to and attending to one of my physical children, so why would I do that to my inner child? Set a regular time to connect with your inner child so you don't get too busy and forget.

Think of this as a commitment to your healing. To break the cycle of nonattuned parenting, neglect, or unavailability, we have to do something different. This is how we break the intergenerational cycles and create a secure inner attachment. Here are some ways to fulfil this commitment. Choose the ones that appeal to you most.

Journaling. You might like to start an inner child journal. This could be a journal for your inner child to draw and write in. Choose something without lines so you have the freedom to be creative and childlike in it.

Inner child meditation. Repeat the meditation in this chapter as often as you like. After a time, you won't need the meditation to get in contact with your child.

Regular check-ins. I recommend starting a daily inner child check-in. The two questions to remember are:

1. How are you?

2. What do you need?

Then go through the three steps of validation, negotiation, and offering described above.

The Joy of Life

Now that you have met your inner child and started to amplify the part of you that is the nurturing parent through the nurturing parent role model, your inner child has access to a different parenting experience. Your child can be cared for and protected by this new nurturing parent, so you can experience more of your inner child's creativity, fun, and joy. If you would like to go deeper with this exploration, you'll find more resources at http://www.psychotherapycentral.health/anxious-attachment.

You now have powerful tools to work with your physical, mental, and emotional bodies. Let's turn to the next chapter, where you'll explore your connection to your spiritual self, reconnect with your ancestors, and engage in powerful healing that gives you a stronger sense of self and belonging.

CHAPTER 5

Spiritual Longing for Compassion and Connection with Ancestors

Your sense of the "spiritual self," the part of you that exists beyond the physical body, can bring feelings of interconnectedness with everyone and everything. You might call this spiritual self your "soul," "Higher Self," or "universal consciousness." This part of you might feel elusive, difficult to get a sense of, and connect with. Or you may have cultivated a strong sense of it. You can think of this part as all-loving, all-knowing, and wise. This chapter offers quite a few exercises because we can't "think" our way into spiritual connection. Spiritual connection happens through the heart. It is a function of love.

With your anxious attachment adaptation, there is often a deep sense of unworthiness, a feeling that your partner is okay, but that you are somehow not okay, that there is something wrong with you. This belief is often rooted in various experiences from your childhood that had nothing to do with who you were, but had more to do with your carer's capacity at the time. As a result, when you connect to aspects of your spiritual self, you are likely to feel you have found part of what has been missing for you: a deeper connection to your essence, something unconditionally loving, being part of something greater, and a place to fall back on when the going gets tough. Over time, connection with this spiritual self will increase your sense of self-worth and inherent value.

There is a growing body of research to back this up, showing a significant connection between spirituality and mental and physical well-being. Increasingly, spirituality and religion are being recognized as contributors to help people successfully "cope with psychological disorders, prevent unhealthy behaviors, and promote resilience" (Elkonin, Brown, and Naicker 2014, 119; Sodhi 2014). An important step toward this is the cultivation of self-compassion.

Self-Compassion Is an Antidote to Self-Criticism

Self-compassion happens when you are present to your own suffering with openness, kindness, nonjudgment, and forgiveness. It is the "capacity to see our struggles with kindly eyes" (Kornfield 2008, 23). Self-compassion is an important concept in the Eastern philosophy of Buddhism, which has increasingly influenced Western psychology in the last thirty years. It is a powerful antidote to self-criticism and self-judgment. In myself and the people in my practice, I notice how much easier it is to have compassion for others than for ourselves.

You likely have an inner parental voice that is critical and sounds like, *You are too noisy, too messy, too needy, too bossy, such a show off.* This is one of the effects of socialization and results in "shame-based self-criticism and self-attacking," which greatly impact well-being (Gilbert 2009, 309). The functional role of self-criticism is to prevent us from repeating a mistake, but often this voice is too loud and harsh.

So how can you dial this voice down? One of the most powerful ways to do this is to let the critical part know that you hear it and understand that it is trying to protect you from making a mistake or being shamed and ask it to step to the side while you bring forward the voice of the *nurturing* inner parent that you discovered in chapter 4. So, if you find yourself being critical of yourself and thinking, *I'm too needy* (something you may have heard a lot as a child), you can invite your nurturing parent in to support your inner child. This might sound like, *You were never "needy" as a child. Of course, you had needs; all children have needs. Your carers were distracted and unable to provide for you in the way you needed them to. It makes sense that you are wanting connection in your relationship now, you are human, and you are allowed to want connection.* Your inner child will often receive these validating and supportive words with relief.

Your nurturing parent might then show the critical parent how their critical words have been affecting the inner child, making the child feel scared, not good enough, or shame. Often, the intention of the critical inner parent is to keep you safe, prevent you from feeling shame, or make sure you get everything done. In the words of Richard Schwartz (2021), there are "no bad parts." You might show the critical parent how you are now taking care of the inner child and they are safe to relax a little.

Offer Yourself Loving-Kindness

The exercise below is one of my favorite meditations. It is a Buddhist practice that can help you connect with your inner well of loving-kindness, giving some of it to yourself to cultivate self-compassion. This form of meditation has been found to result in increased positive emotions, mindfulness, a sense of purpose, better health, a reduction in depression, and an increase in social connectedness (Fredrickson et al. 2008).

This practice has the effect of continually opening the heart. Each time you practice it, you are challenged to stretch your heart open a little more. From an energetic perspective, the energy of the heart is palpable. You might have felt this yourself after a painful breakup when the heart was throbbing with pain or when you felt elated and full of joy and light seemed to emanate from the heart area. When this happens, clients will often say, with some surprise, things like, "My heart feels so alive, open, and full of life, like I can do anything, and there is light coming out of it. Is that normal?" When this happens to my clients, I can usually feel it in my own body because we are connected at that moment.

Loving-Kindness Meditation

I recommend that you make this a daily practice. An audio recording of this practice is available online at http://www.psychotherapycentral .health/anxious-attachment. With time, you won't need to listen to the audio; you'll remember it.

Sit gently upright and rest your hands on your lap.

Notice anything that has been troubling you, relationships or situations, and imagine that you can gently and respectfully place them about ten feet away while you do this practice, clearing a space internally for this meditation.

Become aware of the breath, focusing on the nostrils where the air moves in and out. Bring all your focus to that point. Notice any thoughts, letting them drift over the screen of your mind like a cloud and gently returning to your point of focus. Do this for a minute so you can have time to relax and allow everything to start to slow down. Every time you are distracted, gently return your attention to the breath moving in and out.

When you are ready, follow the breath into the center of your chest, where it naturally meets with the heart space.

Begin with loving-kindness directed toward yourself. Send these blessings to you:

May I be happy. May I be healthy. May I be safe. May I be at peace. Repeat three times.

Recall now someone who has cared for you and repeat the same words to them, sending loving-kindness to them: May you be happy. May you be healthy. May you be safe. May you be at peace. Repeat three times.

Now bring to mind someone with whom you have a neutral relationship and send the same loving-kindness to them: May you be happy. May you be healthy. May you be safe. May you be at peace. Repeat three times.

Now recall a difficult person and send them loving-kindness:
May you be happy. May you be healthy. May you be safe.
May you be at peace. Repeat three times.

Expand your awareness now to all sentient beings (all beings
that feel).

May all beings everywhere be happy and free. Repeat three
times.

Notice any warm sensations in the body that might have
arisen from this practice. Notice any feelings that have
emerged and internally welcome them, knowing this is all part
of the process of the heart softening.

May all beings everywhere be happy and free.

When you are ready, gently move your body and open your
eyes to gaze at the floor before coming fully back.

Remember that you are a sentient being and absolutely deserve love, health, safety, happiness, and peace. No matter what messages you were given as a child, please know that you are worthy of these things. Through the fact of your existence, you deserve love.

When you have a stable core of self-compassion individually, this energy flows out as love and compassion for others, prosocial behavior, charity, generosity, and care for the world we live in, creating compassionate communities (Grof 2003; Leiberg, Klimecki, and Singer 2011). Your spiritual self is another part of you that loves you unconditionally, speaks gently, and is supportive and loving. Your inner child parts love to be cared for by this part of you. You can never be abandoned by your spiritual self, so in times of stress, this part of you can be an invaluable support. This is why cultivating connection with the spiritual self is so beneficial for the anxious adaptation. Spiritual connection can ignite a strong sense of secure attachment and belonging that spreads to all relationships in your life.

Reconnecting with Your Ancestors

The gift of reconnecting with your ancestors is of stepping into the flow of your lineage and proudly taking your place amid your ancestors. You can be supported by the stronger members of your lineage, who you may never have met. In the process, you cultivate a sense of belonging, strength, and different aspects of secure attachment in the relationship with yourself and with your lineage.

As you approach this part of the journey, I'm aware that you may have different feelings about your ancestors. Sometimes there is a sense of connection, and sometimes there is an immediate sense of resistance, anger, or disdain. Perhaps you have spent time thinking about your ancestors, or you may have thought about them very little. Wherever you start from is perfect.

I invite you to step into *imagining* your people. When I use the word "imagining" here, I'm inviting you to imagine your family lineage. This is not what you know rationally about your family, although knowing something can add a dimension to the experience. This is about allowing yourself to sense what is there to be revealed. When sitting with clients doing this ancestral work, I have witnessed deep, profound healing that came with a deeper understanding and experience of their family history.

Exploring Your Lineage

Take some time to think and journal about your family history. Here are some prompts that could be helpful.

- Where are your parents from? What was it like for them growing up?

- Where are your grandparents and great-grandparents from? What do you imagine life was like for them?

- Where are your more distant relatives from? What do you imagine life was like for them?

- What themes run through your family? Is marriage or separation common? Is there adherence to a particular religion? Is there a strong connection to a country or land? Are there themes of suicide, addiction, mental health issues, abuse, adoption, or cutoffs from other family members? What kinds of work do they do? What values do they have? How do they show love and care? How do they deal with conflict and unresolved emotional issues?

You might not know much about your more distant family, but I invite you to imagine what life might have been like for them. In my experience, meaningful insights can emerge from this process.

Connecting with Your Ancestors

In this meditation, you will meet your ancestors. Allow yourself around fifteen minutes to complete this process and the journaling afterward. You might like to light a candle, find some objects that hold sacred meaning, and bring them together to support you in this exploration. It could be as simple as a candle and some shells from a beach that are special to you. An audio recording of this practice is available online at http://www.psychotherapycentral.health/anxious-attachment.

When you are ready, close your eyes, take a deep breath, and gift this time to yourself.

Take another deep breath and let go of anything distracting you, knowing you can return to it after the meditation is complete. Bring your attention to your breath. Notice your chest moving up and down. Gently guide the breath into your belly and begin to notice the subtle sensations in your body. Breathe into any discomfort and let it go. Imagine all tension draining out of your body as you deeply relax.

Become aware of the chair you are sitting on and the feeling of being supported by the chair and the chair being supported by the earth. Become aware of your feet on the earth and the connection through your feet.

You are now going to imagine the land of your ancestors. Notice if you feel pulled to a desert, a lake, a forest, or an open or mountainous area. The area that comes to mind may be a surprise; just flow with whatever comes. Notice what you can see around you. What is the weather like? What can you hear? What can you smell? Notice what it feels like to be in this place and on this land. How does it feel in your body to stand on this land?

Somewhere nearby, you can hear a gathering of your ancestors in a sacred space. Know that you are allowed to approach, that these are your people, your lineage. As you move closer, remember the words of your loving-kindness meditation: "May all beings be happy and free." Send that blessing toward the group as you approach. Notice what you can see, how they are meeting, and in what environment. Is it day or night? Is there a fire or something else as the central focal point? Allow yourself to be welcomed into the group and greeted by one of the elders. This elder sits with you for a time, welcoming you into connection with your ancestry. Notice how the exchange feels for you and what details come through.

When the exchange feels complete, you are given a quality as a gift, something that will be supportive to you moving forward. Notice what quality arrives for you and breathe it in. Notice where it seems to land in your body and how it feels as this quality takes up space inside you.

Thank your ancestors for this meeting with you and for their continued support. When you are ready, start to return to where you came from. From there, start to return to your body by sensing your feet on the floor and your body in the chair. Slowly open your eyes and take in the space around you.

Journal prompts:

- What did the land of your ancestors look and feel like?

- What sense did you get of your ancestors?

- What do you remember about your meeting with the elder?

- What was the quality that you were gifted from your ancestors?

- How did it feel in your body as it was received?

- How might this quality be useful moving forward?

Integration

It is common to feel a lot of power coming from your ancestors, which can be quite a surprise if you have imagined your ancestors to be weak. For most of humanity, surviving has been difficult. Our ancestors have had to survive illness, childbirth, invasion, famine, poverty, and war. Our ancestors were often resilient, resourceful, and in different ways, powerful. Now that you have connected with your ancestors, they are a resource for you. Feel free to revisit them with this meditation as often as you feel is helpful. It can be especially supportive when your anxious tendencies are triggered in relationship. Feeling the support and love of your ancestors will often counter feelings of abandonment, loneliness, and unworthiness.

Resourcing Your Parents

Many of our parents did not have access to the resources and support they needed to be the best parents they could be. Perhaps due to the socioeconomic environment, experiences of marginalization, war, being raised by traumatized parents, or separation from their own parents.

The following exercise is a spiritual process that works on a deep level in the dimension of spirit. This process facilitates intergenerational healing because energy that has been stuck and restricted in the family line is set free through your compassionate engagement with the past. You are able to see how your parents might have been if they had been given the love, attunement, and support they needed in their lives. This softens the heart and allows for more understanding, compassion, and forgiveness toward your parents and ancestors, helping to release the stories of pain you are holding in your body.

These processes also work to alter the inner images of your family that unconsciously influence you into new images that are more supportive and lead you forward in life, allowing you to become unstuck, bringing more empathy with people in your family (Ulsamer 2020). It is common to experience a flood of agency and a sense of wellness that had been absent previously. Take as much time as you need with these exercises and notice any parts of you that might be resistant to imagining your parents as resourced. You might like to remind these parts that this is not about forgetting what happened; this is about releasing some of the pain for you and creating more supportive internal imprints of self and others. If any parts of you are still resistant, you might like to ask them if there is a place where they can feel safe while you do this practice. The scared or angry parts of you might like to wait in your heart or on a beautiful beach, and you can collect them after the exercise.

As this exercise has three parts, you might like to take your time with them and do them over a few days, rather than one after the other in straight succession.

Resourcing Your Mother

Visualization is a tool that's used in spiritual practices in most of the world's major religions. When you visualize in a meditative state, you can receive profound and deeply meaningful insights and inner knowing because you step into a different state of consciousness where new information is available to you. I invite you to step into this exercise with curiosity and to notice the many ways that inner knowing may come to you—through inner vision, inner knowing, your inner voice, felt sensations, and emotions.

As you enter this spiritual realm, you may experience confusion, anger, sadness, joy, or physical sensations. This is common when buried things are revealed; they will express in many different forms and are all part of the healing process. I invite you to trust what emerges and to hold it all and yourself with kindness and compassion.

If you were adopted and are wondering which mother to do this with, I recommend that you do it first with your birth mother and then with your adoptive mother. It doesn't matter if you know nothing about your biological mother when doing this exercise. You will just *imagine* into this space. If you were raised in a family unit without a mother or female caregiver, you might do this exercise first with the person who carried you in their womb and then with the person who most closely felt like your "mother" through your childhood. You can do this practice if your mother has passed away.

An audio recording of this practice is available online at http://www.psychotherapycentral.health/anxious-attachment.

> When you are ready, close your eyes or gently lower them, take a deep breath, and start to turn your attention toward your body and what is happening inside you. Notice the rise and fall of your chest, any areas of tension in your body, and any areas of lightness or that feel softer somehow. Allow all of this to be present.

> Imagine your mother as a baby, in a scene where she is totally wanted, loved, and adored by all her caregivers. You can see she is wanted by the way she is held so gently and the way she is spoken to and cared for. Nothing seems like too much trouble for these parents. They seem to have lots of stability around them, enough money to buy what they need, and safety in their community and country. It is easy for them to put all their attention on your mother, to attune to her, and to meet her needs. Every cell of her body knows implicitly that she is loved and wanted. She belongs and is safe. She knows these parents will protect and care for her until she is an adult.

> Imagine your mother as a toddler growing up with these parents, with them teaching her how to play and interact. Imagine her as a teenager at school with their support. Notice how she seems to be thriving and more confident with these parents in the background supporting her. See her as a young

adult, exploring her identity, enjoying life, and being supported by her environment and the people around her.

Imagine your mother now pregnant with you and having everything she needed to be the best mother she could be. See her with financial support and people around her to help her care for herself and you and see her supported mentally and emotionally in any way she needed.

Imagine yourself being attuned to by your mother, feeling unconditionally loved and wanted, that nothing is too much trouble for her because she has all the energy and resources to be a wonderful mother to you. As you imagine this scene, notice how your body feels. Notice what thoughts are in your mind and what emotions you are feeling.

Spend as long as you like with this scene.

When you are ready, start to reconnect with your body by sensing your feet on the floor and your body in the chair. Slowly open your eyes and take in the space around you.

Journal prompts:

- What was it like to see your mother so well supported as a baby, toddler, teenager, and young adult?

- How did it feel in your body to be attuned to and deeply loved by your mother?

- What thoughts went through your mind as you experienced being cared for in this way?

- What emotions did you feel as you felt your mother's love and support all around you?

Adoption Experience

I was adopted and have never met my birth mother, but I had a powerful, very emotional experience with her during this exercise.

She seemed young and like she wanted to keep me. Imagining her with everything she needed meant she was able to keep me. In that moment, I felt a strong desire to stay with her and found myself in floods of tears—tears of joy that we could stay together and that I was wanted. I had always imagined that my birth mother didn't want me. It was such a surprise. My whole body relaxed into hers, and I felt safe and wanted for the first time in my life. This was so powerful for me.

This is the perfect example of a transformative healing moment, where the energy of being wanted has been blocked, probably since the time of separation from the birth mother. This practice allowed something more life-affirming to emerge. It started to shift this person's model of self, as an unwanted person into a wanted person. If this is true for you too, spend more time with this powerful *imagining* with your birth mother, exploring more deeply what it feels like in your body to be wanted by her, how she might care for you, what thoughts you have when being cared for like this, and exactly what feelings you experience. This will enrich the experience, embed it in your consciousness, and help rewire the plastic brain toward an innate sense of being wanted and worthy.

Resourcing Your Father

If you're not sure who to do this exercise with, follow the same guidelines as in the "Resourcing Your Mother" exercise above: If you were adopted, do it first with your birth father and then with your adoptive father. It doesn't matter if you know nothing about your biological father when doing this exercise. Remember you are just *imagining* into this space. If you were raised in a family without a father or male caregiver, do this exercise with first the person who most closely felt like your "father" through your childhood.

An audio recording of this practice is available online at http://www.psychotherapycentral.health/anxious-attachment.

When you are ready, close your eyes or gently lower them. Take a deep breath and start to turn your attention toward your breath.

Imagine your father as a baby, in a scene where he is totally wanted, loved, and adored by all his caregivers. You can see he is wanted by the way he is gently held and the way he is spoken to and cared for. Nothing seems like too much trouble for these parents. They seem to have lots of stability around them, enough money to buy what they need, and stability in their community and country. It is easy for them to put all their attention on your father, to attune to him, and to meet his needs. Every cell of his body knows implicitly that he is loved and wanted. He belongs and is safe. He knows these parents will protect and care for him until he is an adult.

Imagine your father as a toddler growing up with these parents, with them teaching him how to play and interact. Imagine him as a teenager at school with their support. Notice how he seems to be thriving and more confident with these parents in the background supporting him. See him as a young adult, exploring his identity, enjoying life, and being supported by his environment and the people around him.

Imagine your father being supported while your mother is pregnant with you, so he could be the best father to you. See him with financial support and people around him to help him care for himself and you and see him supported mentally in any way he needed.

Imagine yourself being attuned to by your father, feeling unconditionally loved and wanted, that nothing is too much trouble for him because he has all the energy and resources to be a wonderful father to you. As you imagine this scene, notice how your body feels. Notice what thoughts are in your mind and what emotions you are feeling.

Spend as long as you like with this scene.

When you feel ready, start to reconnect with your body by sensing your feet on the floor and your body in the chair. Slowly open your eyes and take in the space around you.

Journal prompts:

- What was it like to see your father so well supported as a baby, toddler, teenager, and young adult?

- How did it feel in your body to be attuned to and deeply loved by your father?

- What thoughts went through your mind as you experienced being cared for in this way?

- What emotions did you feel as you felt your father's love and support all around you?

Absent Father Experience

I don't know who my father is, but I know I was the result of him having an affair. In the exercise, I imagined him being married to my mother and being a planned child. It was amazing to feel what that would have been like. I got a strong sense that my whole life would have been completely different for me and my mother: more money, playfulness, support, and love. I could feel all this energy in the bottom of my body that made me feel like I could do anything I wanted to.

This is the felt impact of the spiritual healing, where stories and pain held in the body are released and life-affirming energy naturally returns.

Forgiveness

When resourcing your parents, you might find that you become aware of a deeper understanding of their history and struggles, seeing them as people who were dealing with difficult situations and managing their own trauma. You might spontaneously experience compassion or forgiveness for them, which can be surprising.

In my experience, the most powerful way for forgiveness to emerge is through processes like these, where forgiveness emerges almost as a surprise and is not a forced goal. I have seen people try to forgive before they have processed the pain and then battle themselves when anger and hatred resurface. Processing the pain can be done in different ways; you might try some and see what works best for you. It is often a result of a combination of healing approaches. Forgiveness is like a rosebud opening in the sun. If we force it to open too soon, we tear the petals, but if we let it open in its own time, it will bloom in its fullness. Let the bud open in its own time.

Resourcing Yourself

Now it's your turn. Just as your parents may not have had what they needed when they were growing up, neither did you. I have found that when clients see themselves as more resourced, their sense of self starts to change. They feel more capable of handling life, resilient, and more able to have the secure relationships they yearn for.

For many people with the anxious adaptation, the experience of *consistency* is a missing experience. For this reason, as you work on resourcing yourself, focus on the consistency of presence and attunement of your caregivers.

If this exercise brings up a lot of emotion, you might like to pause and take a moment to connect with and care for your inner child as in chapter 4 and return to it another day. An audio recording of this practice is available online at http://www.psychotherapycentral.health/anxious-attachment.

When you are ready, close your eyes or gently lower them. Take a deep breath and start to turn your attention toward your breath.

Imagine yourself as a baby, in a scene where you are totally wanted, loved, and adored by all your caregivers, whether this was your experience or not. Notice the way you are looked at by these loving and tender carers. Notice how they speak to you, how they want to hold you, how they seem to transmit a feeling of their delight in you. Notice what it feels like to be in their presence, to be loved for your presence in their lives. Notice what you feel in your body while you are *being tended to by these loving carers, knowing that they will always be there for you and that nothing you need is too much trouble. Notice what it feels like to feel safe, to be protected, and to belong.*

Imagine yourself now as a toddler, growing up with these caring and supportive people, teaching you how to play and interact with infinite patience. What does it feel like to learn so much, knowing that they are right next to you every step of the way? What does it feel like in your body to know that you can go off and explore and they will be close at hand in case you need them?

Imagine yourself as a teenager at school with their support. Notice how these parents are always in the background cheering you on. See yourself as a young adult, exploring your identity, enjoying life, and being supported by your environment and the people around you.

Spend as long as you like exploring these new scenes.

When you feel ready, you might start to reconnect with your body by sensing your feet on the floor and your body in the chair. Slowly open your eyes and take in the space around you.

Journal prompts:

- What was it like to feel so well supported and loved as a baby, toddler, teenager, and young adult?

- How did it feel in your body to be attuned to and deeply loved?

- What thoughts went through your mind as you experienced being cared for in this way?

- What emotions did you feel as you felt your carers' love and support all around you?

Integration

In this spiritual healing practice, anything can happen. You might find yourself having a missing experience, for example, the experience of being loved, when you never felt loved, or of having parents who were financially stable, when you grew up with a lot of financial insecurity. Notice how having these missing experiences impacts your body and thoughts about yourself.

You might find in this practice that the parents caring for you were not your real parents, but totally different people. It might feel strange but surprisingly good to feel truly wanted and cared for by these new parents. This is not about rejecting your real parents but allowing yourself to experience something different. Trust that the process is moving you in a life forward direction.

If you had some parts that were resistant to this process and have waited patiently for your return, bring them back from where they have been waiting. Show all parts of you what happened through this process and thank them for standing to the side and letting you do this powerful work.

Sacred Healing

This chapter has been an exploration of your spiritual self. You have built on the self-compassion skills that you have been developing through the work you have been doing with the felt sense and the inner child. You have met your ancestors and engaged in the powerful work of resourcing your caregivers, allowing for stuck energy to be organically shifted through your body and your family system. It is possible to stand in the present, bring in missing elements from the past, and change the future.

In the next chapter, you will learn about your nervous system, polyvagal theory, co-regulation, and self-regulation. You will learn how to heal your nervous system by taking manageable steps and allowing your nervous system to have new experiences.

This is powerful healing work. Know that you are doing amazingly well and that I see your bravery in getting this far. Take heart in knowing that there are many others doing this with you at this very moment. Maybe take a moment and feel them. Allow yourself to be supported by them and by me. Know that I see your determination and your heart. Take a moment and breathe in my love and support for you on your journey. I'm so glad you are here doing this work with me.

CHAPTER 6

How Co-Regulation Cultivates Secure Intimacy

You have probably noticed that separations trigger your feelings of abandonment, loneliness, failure, and mistrust. As Lily watches her husband, Amir, drive away to go to work, she feels panic, like she can't breathe properly, and tears well up. Rationally, she knows he is leaving for a good reason and that it is not personal, but there is part of her that feels abandoned and unloved. If you recognize this experience, know that you are not alone. This is common for people with the anxious adaptation because their nervous system is perceiving a threat and is responding to that threat. In this chapter, you will learn about your nervous system and how to ride the waves of activation as they arise.

Regulation and the Nervous System

Our nervous system plays a large role in how we respond to perceived threats, like our partner leaving to go out with their friends for the night. Stephen Porges's (1995) polyvagal theory is a powerful way to understand what happens in our nervous system in everyday situations. We are unconsciously aware through our autonomic nervous system—the part of the nervous system that regulates automatic processes that we don't consciously think about, like heart rate, digestion, and blood pressure. The autonomic nervous system is scanning for danger before we have time to rationally consider the threat, a process called "neuroception" (Porges 2003, 2004).

When you have grown up in unsafe environments, your autonomic nervous system will often respond to things in the present that remind you of people or events from the past. For example, you might be walking down the street, and in your peripheral vision, you see someone walking with your father's gait. Your father was a terrifying man. Without your conscious awareness, your autonomic nervous system senses danger and changes your state from one of calm to one of fight-or-flight. You might feel your heart rate increase, feel panicky in your chest, and have no idea why.

The autonomic nervous system has developed over millions of years. The oldest part of this system is around 500 million years old and called the *dorsal vagal*, which used immobilization to collapse. Perhaps when being outrun by predators, this helped us to look dead. The next system to develop around 400 million years ago was the *sympathetic* response of fight-or-flight, which allowed us to run from predators or fight them. The last system to develop 200 million years ago was the *ventral vagal* ability to connect and have social engagement, which allowed us to find safety through connection with others (Porges 2021). The following table summarizes the three systems.

Neuroception of Safety and Evolutionary Circuit	Function	Experience
Safety: Ventral vagal	Social engagement system: A newer system related to feeling safe and the capacity to engage with others.	Allows connection. Here, we feel safe and can connect with others and experience a range of feelings, including curiosity, joy, interest, wonder, excitement, and compassion. Both right-brain feeling and left-brain reason are functioning. We can be empathic and aware of ourselves.
Danger: Sympathetic	Fight-or-flight behavior, mobilization.	Allows us to take action to fight or run to keep ourselves safe. We focus on self-survival and are hypervigilant. We might feel panicky, jittery, anxious, defensive, or like we want to get away or hit something.
Life-threatening: Dorsal vagal	Shutdown: Ancient and associated with immobilization, dissociation, and collapse.	Causes collapse, reduces blood flow to the brain, resulting in dissociation, and protects us from physical and emotional pain (Porges 2017). It can feel like leaving your body, going numb, or being "checked out." We will often feel "alone, lost, and unreachable. Here is where despair lives" (Dana 2018).

We move through these three states in a predictable way. Beginning in social engagement, if you sense a threat, to protect yourself, you move into fight-or-flight. If you can't fight or run away and the threat is still present, you will enter the shutdown state. This is your amazing nervous system working hard to keep you safe. From shutdown to return to social engagement, you move through fight-or-flight. That is, you bring some energy and activation into the system to return to social engagement.

Daily, you move through these states repeatedly, triggered by large and small events. The aim is not to stay in social engagement all the time, but rather to be able to return to social engagement and not become stuck in fight-or-flight or shutdown. When you can move freely between these states and return to social engagement, you have more resilience when facing the inevitable traumas of everyday living.

The way your autonomic nervous system functions is shaped in early relationships and continues to be influenced by your experiences in adulthood. With the anxious adaptation your primary carer was not attuned *enough*, and there was not *enough* safety, so your incredible body used the sympathetic nervous system to keep your carer close (Cozolino 2002). You might have made huge efforts to be perfect, make them happy, or have big outbursts to get their attention. This is your nervous system trying to keep you safe by keeping your carer close.

When in sympathetic activation, the heart rate increases, breathing is rapid and shallow, and you are hypervigilant. In this state, it is also difficult to read facial expressions to know if someone is safe or unsafe, happy or angry (Dana 2018). When your sympathetic nervous system is consistently activated, you can become stuck in this hypervigilant state, constantly looking for danger, misreading the people around you, and unable to trust bodily felt sensations to know what action to take, resulting in impulsive rather than well-considered action (Ogden, Minton, and Pain 2006). Depending on your lived experience, you might also spend a lot of time in dorsal vagal shutdown. This is often the case when you have experienced childhood trauma.

Because you have not experienced sufficient co-regulation in childhood, moving between the different autonomic states is more difficult, so self-regulation is more challenging than for the securely attached. You are likely to feel shame about some of your impulsive behaviors when triggered, which are a function of your nervous system trying to keep you safe. It is also likely that others have judged you as being "too much" and "needy," often adding to the shame and feelings of low self-worth. It is helpful to remember that when your reaction doesn't match the situation you are in, you have time-traveled, and your younger self is showing up to let you know that they are feeling unsafe and upset.

The good news is that you can learn to become the conductor of your nervous system and over time, gently reshape it and guide it back to experience more regulation. Small moments of being in ventral vagal regulation lead to greater nervous system flexibility, increased self-regulating ability, and increased resilience (Kok and Fredrickson 2010; Dana 2020). For example, you might find that a certain breathing practice helps bring you into ventral vagal regulation, and you remember to use it when you feel yourself entering fight-or-flight to return to a feeling of calm.

When you leave ventral vagal regulation, you have two different ways to come back. The first is using resources that help your body to calm down. We will explore these first. The second is through co-regulation, being with someone you feel safe enough with, who can help you calm down. We will explore this in the second part of this chapter.

Following are two exercises. The first is to identify your triggers and potential resources that might help you when are triggered. The second is to help you track your nervous system state and the impact of the resources you experiment with.

Triggers and Resources

In this exercise you will become aware of the triggers that propel you out of the ventral vagal state. This enables you to plan for potentially triggering events and to set yourself up with the resources you need to support yourself during these times.

Look at the following table and, in your journal, add to the list of triggers that you experience in your life and resources that have worked for you. A useful resource will help your body to calm down. You might yawn or feel lighter, or your shoulders might drop a little. If the practice brings more tension, then it is not the best resource for your body currently. Remember that your nervous system is unique: something that triggers you will not trigger someone else, and what is a wonderful resource for one person is totally unhelpful for another.

	Sympathetic (Fight-or-Flight)	Dorsal Vagal (Shutdown)
Trigger: Things that trigger a movement from ventral vagal to another state.	• Feeling my partner move away from me. • Feeling like I have too much to do. • Going for an interview.	• Seeing someone who was scary when I was a child. • Feeling criticized. • Feeling like I don't belong or am not wanted.
Resources: Things that help me feel safer in my body.	• Talking to my best friend. • Walking in the park. • Breathing in for three and out for six seconds. • Dancing. • Organizing things.	• Noticing my breathing: following the in and out breath. • Any small movement done mindfully. • Smelling a fragrance I like. • Listening to music. • Holding hands with a safe person. • Touching and being touched.

If you'd like more resources for working with triggers and resources, see Deb Dana's book *The Polyvagal Theory in Therapy. Engaging the Rhythm of Regulation.*

Tracking Your Nervous System: Regulation in Practice

To get a better sense of how your nervous system works, it helps to track it. Look at the image below or download it from http://www .psychotherapycentral.health/anxious-attachment and then complete the steps that follow.

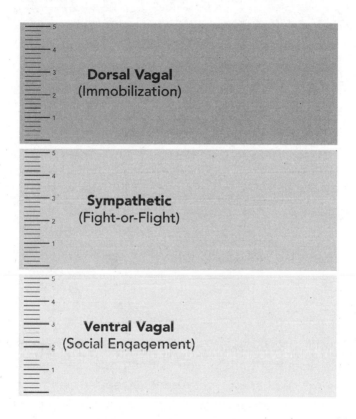

1. Right now, where are you on the nervous system map? For example, it might be that you are in the middle of the sympathetic activation zone.

2. Think about what resource you have that might help you access the ventral vagal state.

3. Allow around five minutes to use that resource.

4. Once complete, reassess your position on the nervous system map and notice what effect that resource had on you.

Your completed nervous system map might look something like this:

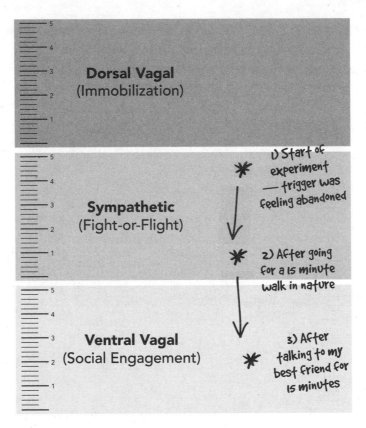

It is useful to do this exercise when you have been triggered so you know what resources work for you to bring more calmness into your body. You will need to use your resources regularly, and with consistency, your nervous system will start to become more regulated, where you are likely to sleep better, have better digestion, have a stronger internal sense of what is safe and unsafe, be able to cope better with stress, and recover from stress more quickly.

Co-Regulation

Humans are wired for connection. Modern neuroscience confirms that the human brain is wired to calm us down by moving closer to people we feel safe with (Coan 2008).

When you have received erratic caregiving, perhaps from a caregiver whose nervous system is stuck in sympathetic activation, it is difficult for your nervous system to know what it *feels* like to be safe and calm. There is no anchor in another person to help lead you into that nervous system state. For this reason, you have likely grown up with little felt sense of feeling safe in your body. You could think of this as a missing experience, something that can be experienced now to create more capacity and flexibility of responses in your nervous system.

Learning co-regulation with another person if you didn't learn it as a child teaches your nervous system what it feels like to be soothed and calmed. You are then able to soothe yourself when you most need it—this is self-regulation. When you can self-regulate effectively, you can calm yourself down faster when distressed and you tend to become less activated. Remember that co-regulating will not leave you dependent on another person; it is filling in the missing experience of co-regulation from your childhood, and with time, this turns into effective self-regulation.

To practice co-regulation, you need to find a trusted other to do it with who spends more time than you in a ventral vagal state (social engagement). Examples might be a therapist you are working with, a good friend, or your partner. Some tips for effective co-regulation include:

- The relationship feels warm and supportive, and you have a sense that the person is there for you and has your back.

- When distressed, the other person moves toward you rather than away, giving empathy and support, providing you are not being aggressive toward them.

- When feeling strong emotions, they may gently remind you of your resources and coping strategies.

- They may help in solving problems and planning for events that are causing stress.

- To allow someone else to help calm your nervous system, explore what the other person does and says that feels calming to you, and let them know so it can become a resource for the future.

When two people are in a close relationship, they can help regulate each other's emotional and physical well-being. Practice the following exercises with a loving partner. You might modify these exercises to do with close friends. Try them when you are both feeling calm, so you can explore which ones could be useful when one of you is feeling distressed. As you experiment with these exercises, you might find them a little uncomfortable. To reshape your nervous system, you need to take manageable steps that stretch you beyond your comfort zone, but don't cause too much stress. This will allow you to have new experiences that imprint new relational safety. I recommend that you experiment with the ones that stand out to you and make the ones that work best for you part of your day-to-day life.

Being with Someone Calm

In this exercise you will explore how it feels to sit with your partner and notice their presence.

1. Sit at a comfortable distance from one another.

2. Bring your awareness to your breath and follow it for around one minute. Simply follow the inhale and exhale.

3. Allow yourself to become aware of your partner's presence.

4. What does it feel like to be in their presence?

5. Notice what thoughts, feelings, and sensations emerge as you sit with them in this calm space.

6. If this feels calming for your body, you might ask your body to remember this experience of being with someone calm.

The Calm Breath

Sit at a comfortable distance from one another or with some physical contact if that feels best for you both.

1. Bring awareness to your breath and follow it for around two minutes.

2. Notice what it is like to focus on your breath in the presence of your partner.

3. Gently start to shift your breathing to a three-six rhythm, where you breathe in for a count of three and out for a count of six.

4. Do this for three minutes and then notice what impact this had on your nervous system state.

Holding Hands

In this exercise, you will explore touch with another safe and calm person. Sit in a position where it will be easy to hold your partner's hand.

1. Bring awareness to your breath and follow it for around two minutes.

2. Move into a position where it is easy to hold hands and it is comfortable for you both.

3. As you hold hands, notice what thoughts, feelings, and sensations emerge as you feel this physical connection.

4. If this feels calming for your body, you might ask your body to remember this experience of being with someone calm.

Remembering Co-Regulation for Self-Regulation

Once you have experienced the soothing effect of another person's nervous system, here are some things you can do to turn that experience into self-regulation.

- When distressed, remember the thoughts, images, and sensations you had when experimenting with the "Being with Someone Calm" and "Holding Hands" exercises.

- Remember the soothing tone of voice and calming things your partner has said to you in the past. Try to replicate that voice as your own self-talk when you feel distressed.

- When activated and alone, you might imagine your partner being close to you, supporting you.

When Lily found herself feeling flooded with emotion, "irrational" thoughts, and panic when her husband left for work, she realized that she was going into a state of sympathetic activation (fight-or-flight). She discussed this with her caring husband, and they decided to practice some of the techniques from this chapter before he left for work. Lily found the "Holding Hands" exercise particularly soothing and connecting. There was something about it that allowed her to feel loved by Amir in a deeper way. She especially liked that he took the time to be with her in this mindful way, even when he was in a hurry. It made her feel important and loved.

Over the next three months, Lily took the time to get to know her nervous system and found that doing yoga and breathing exercises in the morning and planning for triggering events were powerful self-regulation tools. As Amir and Lily explored the techniques in this chapter, Lily found that her separation anxiety calmed substantially. She was surprised that Amir had been willing to offer her so much understanding and tenderness as she experienced co-regulation, and that experience had led her into more self-regulation and self-trust.

The Gift of Self-Regulation

In this chapter, you learned about different nervous system states. You have taken the time to explore the triggers that propel you out of social engagement and into sympathetic or dorsal vagal states. You also gathered some effective resources to help you return to a state of calm. In the second part of the chapter, you explored the power of co-regulation and how this helps create self-regulation. In the next chapter, you will move deeper into relationship dynamics to explore common relationship blocks for the anxious adaptation and how to deal with them. The tools you have gathered from chapters 1 to 6 are the new practices you will bring into your relationship and are the foundation for building your secure relationship.

CHAPTER 7

Reaching Out for Connection

Have you ever reached out for connection with your special person and felt desperate? It might feel like panic in your belly or chest and terror that you will be left hanging, alone. You might worry that they will push you away with their body, with a look, or with their words. You want to stay close to them and be seen, loved, and met, but you feel like you are too much or needy and that they want more space than you in the relationship. And it hurts like crazy.

You might be wondering why you seem to end up with people on the avoidant end of the attachment spectrum again and again, getting hurt and having another failed relationship to add to the list. Because the anxious-avoidant dynamic between people is so common and causes so much pain, we are going to spend some time on this topic.

As we move into the relational section of this book, it is important to note that if you are in an abusive relationship (a relationship where there is sexual, emotional, physical, or financial abuse, or controlling behavior, where your partner puts you down or threatens you), it is essential you reach out for support by calling a domestic violence helpline. The exercises offered in this book are for couples who have a foundation of safety and mutual respect in their relationship.

The Dance of the Anxious-Avoidant Couple

When you have grown up with inconsistent caregiving, part of you will find an inconsistent connection in a relationship familiar and attractive, even though it is uncomfortable. You are likely to find yourself drawn to people with a more avoidant style because they are inconsistent in their love, affection, and availability. No matter how painful it might feel, some aspects of this behavior are familiar, and we tend to be drawn to what we know.

This makes sense when you remember the inconsistent love, attention, and care that was given to you as a child. When you reached for comfort, sometimes you were responded to, and sometimes you were ignored, sent away, told that you were annoying, and left to comfort yourself. This builds an internal model of others, or expectation of others, as unreliable. It makes love and care unreliable. As a child, it is natural to assume this erratic caregiving is a result of your lack of lovability. In your child's mind, because the drive to attach to the caregiver is so strong, if the caregiver is violent or erratic, you will assume it is because of something you did or something wrong with you. This becomes internalized as your model of self—how you expect people to respond to you because of who you are deep down—affecting your self-esteem and self-worth.

With time, you can change these internal models of self and others. You have already started to powerfully work on your model of self in the first six chapters of this book. In this chapter, we will explore the anxious-avoidant relational pattern, how it evolves, and how to move into a more secure relational pattern.

When a secure attachment is missing in childhood, there are two ways to deal with the fears and attachment needs that arise in a relationship:

1. Avoidant adaptation: Avoid the emotion by shutting down (for example by being cold or aloof or withdrawing).

2. Anxious adaptation: Increase the emotion and try to get a response (for example by making threats, becoming increasingly demanding, or nagging).

Avoidant Attachment

To fully understand the anxious-avoidant dynamic, it is useful to understand the avoidant attachment adaptation you are attracted to. The avoidant pattern largely comes from "consistent and repetitive rejection of the child's attachment behaviors" (Brown and Elliott 2016, 107). Imagine a child reaching up for their parent, desperate to be seen and held, and the parent, feeling resentful, numb, depressed, or tired, turning away. These parents don't tend to enjoy physical contact and will avoid it. The child's efforts to connect are met with emptiness, disdain, neglect, or punishment.

In response, the child makes fewer efforts to connect. They become more self-reliant and suppress their relational needs because they learn that those needs are unimportant or result in punishment and rejection. They develop a false sense of independence at the expense of connection. They learn that connection is not a warm and nurturing place but a cold and rejecting experience they would rather avoid. Avoidantly attached adults:

- find intimacy uncomfortable

- find it difficult to trust others

- have a drive to be independent and value self-reliance

- find emotions difficult, in themselves and others

- are often disconnected from their needs

- find it difficult to ask for help and be vulnerable

- don't worry about being abandoned

- manage distress by cutting off feelings

- are often found to be distant and cool by partners

- find themselves shutting down in conflict or saying whatever they think the other person wants to hear.

Under the hurt, most avoidant people want to be in a relationship, but it is terrifying for them. They have been wired to expect rejection. On the more extreme end of the avoidant spectrum, the avoidantly attached person may feel they don't need relationships. They are cut off from their feelings and find the feelings of others uncomfortable or weak. They find it challenging to open up to their partner, even when they want to, because historically, it hasn't been safe.

Partners might find their avoidant partner cold and rejecting and end up feeling alone in the relationship. As the partner of someone with avoidant tendencies, you likely feel the wounded inner child inside of them. You keep hoping that the shutdown adult will open up. If you had a caregiving role as a child, you may find yourself in a similar dynamic where you are drawn to "fix" your partner, often an exhausting exercise.

When You Dance Together and It Hurts

If you have been in a relationship for more than two years, it is likely that you noticed some repeating patterns in your disagreements that leave you feeling farther apart. Sue Johnson (2008), the creator of Emotionally Focused Therapy (EFT), a therapy that puts attachment needs at the center of all intimate relationships, has identified one of the main patterns played out in distressed relationships as the pursuer-withdrawer dynamic. In this dynamic, the pursuer has anxious patterns, and the withdrawer has avoidant patterns. She views each person's role in the cycle as their best attempt to meet their attachment needs: to feel loved, appreciated, and accepted.

Jan noticed the same repeating pattern seemed to be happening whenever she and her partner, Ben, had a disagreement, regardless of what it was about. The most recent disagreement had gone like this: Unexpectedly, Ben found that he had to do some work while they were away on a short family vacation. When Jan found Ben in the bedroom working, she was really disappointed because she wanted Ben to be with the family that weekend. She began complaining to Ben, who defended his need to work for just a few hours. Jan said that this always happens, that he tries to hide from her and the kids by working. Ben felt attacked and wanted the fight to end, so he closed the laptop and went to watch TV with the kids. They managed not to have a full-blown fight, but the disagreement tainted the weekend. Jan was left with an unsettled feeling and sadness. Ben was left feeling like he was in trouble and a failure again, shutdown, and distant.

This is the pattern: Jan feels strongly about something that Ben disagrees with. Jan becomes "loud and pushy" and goes into fight-or-flight because she has sensed danger in the relationship. She feels anxious and vulnerable. She is trying to get his attention and agreement so they can move closer together again.

Ben becomes defensive. He might become logical as a way to defend himself. As Jan protests more, Ben eventually gives up to avoid any further conflict, leaving him feeling defeated and resentful. Ben withdraws into himself and becomes distant. Ben has learned to shut down to avoid feeling pain. He naturally does this with Jan to avoid feeling hurt, disapproval, or rejection. Ben is trying to protect the relationship by stopping the argument.

As Ben withdraws, Jan senses more danger to the relationship, so her automatic reaction is to pursue Ben. She tells Ben that he is cold and that she wonders why she is staying in the relationship. Jan desperately wants Ben to turn toward her and connect with her. She is expressing anger, but underneath the anger, her more vulnerable feelings are loneliness and sadness.

Ben feels Jan's anger intensely and wants to get away. Ben feels criticized and judged and just wants the argument to stop, so he represses his feelings, shuts down, and withdraws even more.

Here's how the cycle usually plays out:

1. Pursuer: *Protesting lack of closeness, I complain, get bigger, and criticize.*

2. Withdrawer: *I feel attacked and criticized, so I shut down; become dismissive, defensive, or logical; or focus on tasks.*

3. Pursuer: *When I feel you move away, my alarm bells go off, and I become more distressed. I protest more to try to get your attention.*

4. Withdrawer: *The more you protest, the more I shut down and withdraw.*

This dance leaves you feeling frustrated, more distant, helpless, unloved, and disconnected. You wonder why you bother. You feel confused by your partner's reaction and interpret it as them not caring for you or the relationship. This is a common dance. Know that you can learn how to break this cycle and create the intimacy you yearn for in your relationship. Let's understand more about both the protest and withdrawer behaviors and what they are trying to achieve.

Protest Behaviors Are a Call for Connection

When a secure attachment is missing, one of the ways to deal with this lack of safety is to avoid the emotion, as we have seen with the avoidant adaptation. The other strategy you will likely recognize in yourself to deal with this disconnect is increasing emotion. This isn't something that you plan for; it's an automatic reaction. Sue Johnson (2008) says, "When we get no emotional response from a loved one, we are wired to protest" (75). This protest can take different forms, and you are likely to have a few that you automatically default to. At their core, protest behaviors are a frantic effort to receive comfort, alleviate fears of being abandoned, and ultimately reconnect. However, you have probably noticed that the impact often pushes the other person away and leaves you feeling more alone and sometimes in a pit of shame. You will notice that you use these protest behaviors when your attachment system has been activated and your nervous system has gone into fight-or-flight. Protest behaviors might include (Levine and Heller 2010; Mikulincer and Shaver 2016; Kallos-Lilly and Fitzgerald 2022):

- repeated texting or calling when distressed

- becoming increasingly demanding

- sulking—withdrawing your energy from the relationship as punishment

- threatening to leave the relationship

- getting in touch with an ex to make your partner feel jealous

- acting more vulnerable, ill, or needy than you are

- questioning, nagging, attacking

- blaming, criticizing, judging

- demanding, confronting, attacking, yelling, pushing the other to respond.

Withdrawing Behaviors Try to Protect the Relationship

It is often a shock for those of you with the anxious adaptation to hear what is going on for your avoidant partner when they withdraw. I remember being in counseling with my husband and describing a scene where I had been distressed and emotional about something going on at work. I wanted him to see my point of view, to be my safe haven, to metaphorically embrace me and hold me. Instead, he stood in the other person's shoes and described what might be happening for them. He got rational and remained objective. Not understanding why, I felt betrayed and hurt by this response; it didn't feel like he was in my corner.

When he reflected on the scene, my husband said he could see that I was distressed and wanted to help. The best way he thought he could help was to explain what might be happening for the other person. That seemed logical to him and something that he would find helpful if he were in my situation. This was him genuinely caring for me. When he described his intention, I could see the mismatch and feel his care for me. I didn't have the language or understanding to be clear about what I needed from him in that moment, and he didn't have the automatic programming to step toward me with empathy and emotional connection. I was left feeling unsupported, and he was left feeling like he had somehow got it all wrong.

As a naturally empathic person, I am usually very aware of what is happening for the other person and struggle to separate what is mine and what is theirs. When I am distressed, I need my partner to be with me, to support me, and to be empathic with me, rather than with the other person. This might have sounded like, "Wow, that sounds full-on. Know that I'm here for you and that you are doing your best in a difficult situation. I'm happy to brainstorm with you if that would be helpful or just listen and be with you." If he had said something like that, you can be sure I would have said, "Yes, please just listen and share my experience. We can brainstorm later." I needed to be heard and held with genuine love and care, something I know he is capable of.

Now, this doesn't mean that a rational response is always the "wrong" response. Sometimes a rational response is absolutely the best, but in moments of high emotion, it is likely to fall flat and leave the anxious partner feeling unsupported, uncared for, and their experience minimized.

The subtext of the withdrawing behaviors in the avoidant adaptation is often a fear of emotion and conflict. When you get emotional, they are likely to have an automatic shutdown response that is them trying to fix the problem and make it go away, to calm you down as quickly as possible, in a way that probably works for them, but leaves you feeling unheard, alone, and dismissed. The impact of them shutting down, getting logical, or minimizing the issue inadvertently pushes you away, causing more disconnection, whereby you protest more, and the cycle continues. Withdrawing behaviors might include (Kallos-Lilly and Fitzgerald 2022):

- getting logical and problem-solving
- dismissing or minimizing the issue
- becoming defensive
- shutting down, not feeling anything, withdrawing
- going silent and walking away
- agreeing with whatever you say to keep the peace.

How to Do a Different Dance

The key to changing the dance you do as a couple with this relationship pattern is to connect with the emotions and attachment needs that lie hidden underneath the behaviors. This is the foundation of Sue Johnson's

(2008) Emotionally Focused Therapy. Vigorous research shows that 70 to 75 percent of distressed couples that go through EFT recover and are able to create happy relationships (Johnson 2008). EFT is done with a therapist who can act as a temporary support and attachment figure for the couple, especially when there has been betrayal and other attachment wounding in the relationship. As a couple, consider what your attachment needs are. No matter how deeply buried they are, we all have emotions, attachment needs, and fears underneath protest, withdrawal, criticism, or shutdown. Attachment needs include:

- the need to be understood and accepted

- the need to feel loved, wanted, and important to your partner

- the need to know your partner will be there when you need them

- the need to feel close to your partner, like the two of you are a team

- the need to feel appreciated.

Attachment fears include:

- you won't be enough for your partner and will be rejected and abandoned

- you're flawed and will be too much for your partner

- when you need your partner, they won't be there, and you'll be alone

- you'll end up being controlled by your partner.

It is useful to keep these lists close by as you delve into the emotions and attachment needs that are the fuel for many of your painful interactions.

Discovering Your Core Emotions and Attachment Needs

When you are in touch with your core emotions and attachment needs, it is easier to know what your needs are and to ask for them. Using your journal, think of a recent disagreement and work through the table below (Johnson 2008; Herbine-Blank, Kerpelman, and Sweezy 2016; Kallos-Lilly and Fitzgerald 2022). A blank version of this table is available online at http://www.psychotherapycentral.health/anxious -attachment.

1	**Event:** What happened factually	My partner told me she is going out with her friends for the third night this week.
2	**Meaning making:** What I made this mean	My partner doesn't really want to be with me. I'm at the bottom of the pile.
3	**Behavior:** What I did	I became critical and upset. I told her maybe we should break up.
4	**Expressed emotions**	Anger, frustration, and hopelessness.
5	**Core emotion:** The emotion that lives under the expressed emotion and is often more vulnerable	Deep down I felt sad, alone, and unsure if my partner loves me.
6	**Attachment needs**	I needed to feel loved and important.

Tracking a Negative Cycle

When you are both calm, connected, and curious, in social engagement, and feel you have space, explore what happens for you and your partner during conflict. It is easier to start with something that actually happened so you can both go back in time and think about what was happening for each of you. This is a vulnerable conversation because you are both going to examine your behavior, core emotions, and attachment needs.

In this exercise, you are tracking your "negative cycle." A negative cycle is a repetitive pattern of interaction that happens regardless of the subject being discussed. This kind of tracking was developed in early family therapy to explore patterns of behavior (Minuchin and Fishman, 1981). Showing your partner the table below will probably make you both feel a little safer as you likely see your pattern written out and know that you are not alone in this dynamic. The result might look something like this:

		Pursuer Patterns (Anxious Adaptation)	Withdrawer Patterns (Avoidant Adaptation)
1	**Event:** What happened factually	My partner told me she is going out with her friends for the third night this week.	I told my partner I had to go out tomorrow for a friend's birthday.
2	**Meaning making:** What I made this mean	My partner doesn't really care about me. I'm at the bottom of the pile.	I'm not allowed to go out with my friends. I never get it right. I'm always in trouble.

		Pursuer Patterns (Anxious Adaptation)	Withdrawer Patterns (Avoidant Adaptation)
3	**Behavior:** What I did	I became critical and upset. I told her maybe we should break up.	When my partner became critical, I felt attacked. First I tried to reason and defend, and then I withdrew to my bedroom.
4	**Expressed emotion**	Anger, frustration, and hopelessness.	I shut down and withdrew.
5	**Core emotion:** The emotion that lives under the expressed emotion and is often more vulnerable	Deep down I feel sad, alone, and unsure if my partner loves me.	Deep down I'm scared of conflict and of disappointing my partner.
6	**Attachment needs**	I need to feel loved and important.	I need to feel loved and appreciated.

You can download a blank copy of this table at http://www.psycho therapycentral.health/anxious-attachment.

Cycle Breaking Version 1: Pursuer Changes the Way They Engage

Whenever you have identified a cycle—a repeating pattern in your life, family, or relationship—that is unhelpful and you decide to do something different, you are breaking a cycle. Below are examples of what it looks like to sustain a cycle and break it. Compare the following approaches that Jan tried.

Cycle Sustaining

Jan: *This always happens: You try to hide from me and the kids by working. You're never here, even when we're on a vacation. I feel so angry.*

Here, Jan is sharing her "expressed emotion." She is using "always" and "never" generalizing language that has the effect of putting the other person on the defensive. She is not in touch with her core emotion or attachment need.

Cycle Breaking

Jan: *I know work is really demanding and hard to let go of and that you are working to support us all, but I really wanted you to have a break from it this weekend. I feel lonely with just the kids all the time. I really want to spend some time with just the two of us. I need to feel that I'm important to you.*

In the second version, Jan is in touch with and has expressed her core emotion and attachment needs and has given Ben a clear request to help them move forward. Because Jan is more vulnerable and less threatening, it is easier for him to respond to her in a different way. In this way, the cycle is changed.

Cycle Breaking Version 2: Withdrawer Changes the Way They Respond

Compare the following scenarios:

Cycle Sustaining

Jan: *This always happens: You try to hide from me and the kids by working. You're never here, even when we're on vacation. I feel so angry.*

Here, Jan is attacking and critical, using "always and never" language.

Ben: *I knew you were going to be angry, that's why I hid up here. I've been with you and the kids all day; this is just a few hours; you are totally overreacting.*

Ben is defensive, logical, and minimizing. Because Jan's attachment needs are not met, she is likely to escalate.

Cycle Breaking

Ben hears Jan's anger as an attachment protest, a cry for connection. Ben resists his impulse to be defensive and respond to the expressed emotion of anger. Rather, he imagines what the deeper core emotion and *attachment need* might be: "I'm guessing that me being here is making you feel *lonely?*" He stands up and moves toward Jan to give her a hug. "I'm sorry. You are so important to me. I guess I started to feel anxious about work again and that took over, I'm sorry." Jan is likely to feel seen and cared about from this interaction, even though her approach was attacking. Her attachment need is being met, and she is likely to soften. The cycle has been diffused.

Changing patterns is not easy. In my experience it takes courage and practice, practice, practice. It also helps if you can get your partner on board. Perhaps they can read this chapter of the book so you can both get a clear picture of the cycle in your relationship and how to change it. This is powerful work because when we reach out for connection in a different way and are met with increased intimacy, we are rewiring our attachment pattern to be more secure. We begin to see the other as more reliable, supportive, and loving, and we start to see ourselves as being more worthy of love, appreciation, and attention.

Tips for the Avoidants

Avoidants can heal by spending time connecting with and identifying their emotions. They need to practice moving toward their partner when they see distress and resist the urge to withdraw or shut down (unless their partner is being violent or abusive). Here are ways avoidants can soothe an anxious partner:

- Avoid problem-solving and getting too logical. When your partner is distressed, they need to be soothed and supported first to feel that you are with them emotionally. Problem-solving might be useful later.

- You might ask what your partner is needing from you. They might want to be held, need to be heard, or want to be understood. This can help your partner get clear about what they need from you too.

- Use the co-regulation strategies in "Being with Someone Calm," "The Calm Breath," and "Holding Hands" exercises from chapter 6.

- Validate their distress. Emotional pain isn't something to be eradicated as soon as possible. It is often carrying an important message and is moved through faster with compassion and support rather than logic. Try understanding why they might be feeling so distressed. What context might be relevant? This might sound like, "It makes sense that you would find this so upsetting…. I'm wondering how I can support you or what you might need from me right now. I can hear how distressing this is; know that I'm here for you through this." Remember that validating a feeling or experience doesn't mean you are agreeing with them, just that you are validating their emotion and attempting to understand it in context and give it space. This often has the effect of calming the other person because they feel heard and understood.

Changing How You Engage as the Pursuer

Research has found that the first three minutes of a conflict discussion accurately predict the likelihood of divorce (Carrère and Gottman 1999). A soft startup is one of the keys to better conflict. A soft startup is one where you have a legitimate complaint but avoid blaming or criticizing, which puts your partner on the defensive, and you try to use "I" rather than "you" statements.

You might read these out loud to get a feel for the difference.

Harsh startup. "You are always home late. I think you do it on purpose to avoid having to bathe the kids. You leave it all to me." (Note the expression of anger, blame, criticism, and judgment.)

Soft startup. "I feel sad and lonely when you come home late. I would love for us to eat and then bathe the kids together. Do you think you would be able to do that one day this week?" (Notice the use of "I" statements and the connection to the core emotions of sadness and loneliness. There is no judgment, and a need is clearly expressed.)

Harsh startup. "You never stand up to your parents. You let them push us around, and I'm fed up with it."

Soft startup. "I feel abandoned and sad when we have these issues with your parents. I imagine that you are trying to keep the peace and it's difficult for you. I wonder if we could talk about it and come together on this issue?"

What Does a Secure Relationship Look Like?

Now that you have examined your past experiences in relationship, let's discuss what a secure relationship looks like. It is worth noting that the research indicates that it takes about two years to develop a secure relationship (Zeifman and Hazan 2016). While the relationship is developing, friends and family still play an important role, with that role decreasing significantly after two years.

Here are the qualities of a secure relationship:

- Your partner is a *safe haven* for you. When you are with them, you feel safe and secure; reassurance and comfort are freely given.

- Your partner is a *secure home base* for you. You spend time together and apart. When you go off to have new experiences, they support you to do that. You feel more courageous knowing they are there for you should you need them.

- Both people in the relationship provide and receive love, care, and nurturance in a fairly balanced way.

- There is sexual activity that strengthens the bond.

Here's what secure attachment *feels* like:

- *I can rest in the knowledge that my special person is there for me when issues come up.*

- *There is a sense that my feelings are valid and given space, even when we might disagree.*

- *I trust my partner.*

- *We can both express our needs, and all needs are given equal weight in the relationship.*

- *We can support each other emotionally when it's needed.*

Creating a New Relationship Template

When we haven't experienced a secure relationship, it can be difficult to imagine what one would feel like. This exercise helps create new neural pathways that will anchor a new relational experience and set up the tendency to look for different things in a potential partner (Brown and Elliott 2016). An audio recording of this practice is available online at http://www.psychotherapycentral.health/anxious-attachment.

Take a moment to notice your surroundings, and gently close or lower your eyes when you feel ready. Take a deep breath with a long exhale and then turn your awareness inward. We are going to take this time to create a new relationship template.

Imagine that you are arriving home to someone who loves you deeply. If you are in a committed relationship, have this person be your partner. If you are not, have it be someone you have never met. Notice that they greet you with warmth and love; they light up as they see you enter the house.

There is something about this person that is incredibly safe and gives a sense that they will protect you, that they have your back. Notice what that feels like in your body. Because you love and care for them, you can feel a sense of protectiveness toward them too.

This person is attuned to you. They notice how you might be feeling, and there is a sense that all your feelings are heard and welcome. There is no part of you that is not welcome. As you relax into that thought, notice how it feels in your body to be completely accepted just as you are. You are also attuned to them, and you notice how they might be feeling and make space for those feelings in return.

If either of you is distressed, it is natural for the other person to come forward to soothe the other, letting you know that they are there for you, that they are not going anywhere, that you are safe and cherished, and that you are enough. There is a wonderful feeling of both being cherished and cherishing the other person. As you expand this vision, notice how your body is responding.

In this secure relationship, there's lots of laughter and joy; there is space for you to both grow and learn, to go off and learn new things and meet new people, to express yourselves in different ways, and to return to the safety and comfort of the relationship.

Take a moment to enrich this image, to imagine what it might be like to be held by this person who adores you, to go on adventures together, to face life's challenges as a team. Notice how your body feels as you imagine this secure, nourishing relationship.

Take a moment to thank the vision and your mind and body for participating.

When you feel ready, open your eyes and look slowly to the left and then the right, noticing a few things in the space around you. Then add in some gentle movement that helps to anchor you fully in your body.
Take some time to journal your experience with this exercise.

The Dance of the Anxious and Avoidant

In this chapter, we explored common relationship struggles for the anxious adaptation as well as some of the relational issues that come with reaching out for connection for both the anxious and avoidant styles. We unpacked the dance of these attachment styles and the protest and withdrawal that is so common as well as different ways to break this destructive cycle. You then reviewed what a secure relationship feels like before having your own experience of one. Understanding this common relationship dynamic will help you in chapter 8 as you explore what happens for you when you are triggered in a relationship.

When Your Anxiety Is Triggered in Relationship

Rose knew that she had an anxious adaptation and that her partner, Maggie, had a more avoidant attachment style. Rose noticed Maggie would pull away when she reached out for connection by holding hands in public. Rose found it hurtful, especially when they were out with friends when she needed a bit of reassurance, a little gesture that says, "You are safe, I'm your person, and we are together." Rose had mentioned that she liked to hold hands in public, but Maggie had said she didn't like any public displays of affection.

On Saturday night, Rose was feeling a little insecure because one of Maggie's exes was present. Rose had reached out for reassurance a few times, trying to make eye contact and making a few jokes. When she got no response, she put her arm around Maggie. When she did, she felt Maggie's body tense. Rose thought, *I might as well not be here*, and left the party without saying good-bye. Part of Rose was hoping that Maggie would follow, but she didn't. Then she started to send Maggie a flurry of angry texts about what a cold person she was. When she didn't get a quick response, she suggested they should break up, the opposite of what she wanted.

In this example, Rose had reached out for connection and felt rejected. She needed reassurance about the relationship and didn't receive it. This triggered Rose's anxious patterns, and she became reactive and moved into protest behaviors—angry texts and threatening to leave—which only left her feeling panicky and unable to calm down. You likely recognize scenarios like this one. There is a saying, "If it's hysterical, it's historical." This means the trigger is likely to have its origin in the past.

What Are Your Relationship Triggers?

A trigger is when something happens and we have an emotional reaction that seems stronger than the situation calls for. It might be when your husband refuses to put your son to bed and you feel let down, alone with the task of parenting and overwhelmed. It might be a feeling of your partner prioritizing their family over you, which leaves you feeling second best and wondering if you are enough.

Triggers are caused by implicit memory (nonverbal and unconscious, for example images, emotions, beliefs, and patterns related to events we don't remember) or explicit memory (remembering what happened in what order). What has happened to us in past relationships influences future relationships and how we expect the world to be. We only remember these experiences through current relationships when we respond to people with anger or neediness and have no idea why.

I invite you to think of your triggers as treasures because they are a powerful way of getting to know yourself. Something has happened that has caused your internal alarm system to go off. This is a moment to be curious and kind toward yourself.

Healing Triggers

Triggers can be a doorway to deep healing, if you are conscious of their presence and choose to address them. The exercise below is the foundation of a powerful healing practice that can be repeated again and again. In this process, you are guided into the past to heal the source of the trigger, often a childhood wound. There is also a powerful opportunity to connect with your younger parts and build a more secure internal attachment.

Trigger Healing

In your journal, think of a recent trigger you would like to understand more deeply.

1. What happened? Trigger.

   He didn't call when he knew he was going to be late.

2. What did you feel in your body?

   I felt tight in my stomach and panicky in my chest.

3. What did you make it mean?

   He doesn't want to be with me. He's just not there. He doesn't care about me.

4. What was the core emotion? The one that lives under the one that is expressed and is often more vulnerable.

   Deep down, I felt sad, disappointed, alone, and unsure if he loves me.

5. When do you remember feeling this way? Let yourself remember where you were and what was happening. Let your mind roam and trust the first image or sensation that arises. (Note: If you land in a deeply frightening and unsafe place, then this is an exercise to do with a professional who is trained in trauma therapy).

   This is how I felt when I was seven years old and sent away to boarding school. I see myself clinging to my mother as she left me on the first day. I feel teary as I remember it.

6. What did you need then that you didn't get?

   I needed to know it was going to be okay.

   What would you say to your younger self?

   I'd let her know that it would be okay, but if she would prefer to come and live with me, I'd love that.

How is it for your younger self to hear this?

She is so relieved. She feels wanted and loved and is keen to live with me.

When your younger self has finished sharing with you, allow your child to gently step inside your heart where they are safe and loved.

7. Think about the original trigger, sense if its charge has changed, and check the initial bodily sensations.

    When I think about him not calling, I want to talk to him about it, but I don't feel nearly as distressed as I did before. The sensations in the stomach and chest have gone.

8. What is your *attachment need* that you could share with your partner?

    I need to feel loved and wanted.

9. What do you *need*?

    I'd love you to call when you are going to be late. This would help me to feel loved and important to you.

Future Triggers

I often hear clients talking about things in the future they are dreading. They already know what is going to happen and how they are going to respond. When this is the case, planning ahead can make all the difference. It is a powerful form of self-care for you and your relationship.

Planning for Future Triggers

In your journal, take some time to plan for future triggers.

1. Anticipated trigger and feeling.

    My partner is going to a work function with many interesting people and alcohol. I know I will feel anxious and scared that he will meet someone else.

2. How do I usually react?

I feel distressed and angry with him, so I usually pick a fight. I can't help myself. Then while he's out, I'll text or call him frantically for reassurance.

3. What else could I do?

a. I could let him know that I'm feeling anxious and that being alone is a trigger for me from my childhood. I could ask him if he would be willing to send me a few texts while he's there, so I know he is thinking about me.

b. I could arrange to spend the night with my friend, so I'm distracted and in connection with someone who cares about me.

c. I could spend the evening meditating and doing yoga and then watching a peaceful movie.

4. How might these other options bring different results? How might they feel in your body, mentally and emotionally?

a. If I let him know what I need, he might do it, and that would feel softer in my heart area and reassuring mentally and emotionally.

b. Staying with a friend would be distracting. When I think about that, I feel light in my upper chest and more grounded. I feel happy, and my mind is clearer.

c. I feel grounded and peaceful when I imagine staying home and doing meditation and yoga. Although thoughts of him pop up, my mind generally feels calm, and I'm more able not to be overwhelmed by negative thoughts.

5. Which option feels like the best one for this specific trigger?

Pausing During Conflict

With the anxious adaptation, you are probably not used to pausing during conflict. There is a fear that the conflict will not be resolved if you pause and that there will be distance in the relationship that might lead to separation. Not pausing might lead to you both becoming more escalated and saying things you later regret. Taking a break can protect the relationship bond but takes a bit of practice.

Sure signs that you need to take a break during a difficult conversation are:

- you have become reactive

- you are repeating yourself

- you have shut down

- you are interrupting them to defend yourself

- you are being disrespectful and saying things you will later regret

- you have stopped deeply listening

- you have become shaming or threatening

- you have become violent, physically or with your words.

When in conflict, it is common that your nervous system has left social engagement and entered sympathetic activation (fight-or-flight) or dorsal vagal (immobilization). To bring yourself back into regulation, you first need to know that you have left social engagement and then give yourself some time and resources to return.

Rupture and repair can be powerful catalysts for growth in your relationship. Reminding yourself that conflict is part of relationships and that the magic is in the repair can be helpful. When a conflict is repaired, it doesn't mean that the issue being discussed has necessarily been resolved. It means the emotional connection has been reestablished or never lost during the disagreement. When you can safely disagree with one another and stay connected, you build more trust and intimacy.

Seven Steps to a Successful Pause

Here are seven steps for pausing during a conflict. You can use these steps as a couple to practice your pausing skills, to get to know yourself better, to share more vulnerably with your partner, and to practice rupture and repair.

Step 1. Noticing

Notice that you are being reactive or defensive or feeling upset. Notice how it feels in your body. This sounds like, *I'm feeling so angry right now that I can feel a lot of energy in my arms, and my head wants to explode.*

Step 2. Ask for a Break

Let your partner know you are overwhelmed and need to take a pause. *"I know this is important, but I feel like we are repeating ourselves, and this conversation isn't going anywhere. I need to take a break and walk for twenty minutes to clear my head, and then I'll be in a different place to work this out with you."* It is helpful to put a time limit on the pause to prevent avoidance of the issue.

Step 3. What Do I Need?

Ask yourself what you most need right now. It might be a glass of water, to get out of the house, or to do some deep breathing. You might check in on your inner child, as you learned in chapter 4, or practice some somatic bodywork through the Focusing practice you learned in chapter 2 ("The Six-Stage Focusing Practice"). You might look at the resources you developed, in the "Triggers and Resources" exercise in chapter 6, and choose one to use now.

Step 4. Identify the Core Emotion

Under the anger, I am feeling sad. Once accessed, try to stay in contact with the core emotion. It will help you express vulnerability when you come back together.

Step 5. Apologize if Required

Return to your partner and apologize for your regretful behavior or speech. *"I'm sorry I yelled at you. That wasn't okay. I want to create more safety when we disagree. I'm committed to not yelling as we discuss this more."*

Step 6. Reconnect

Every relationship has subtle ways of reconnecting after a disagreement. Here are some common ones. In your journal, write down which ones you would like to use and others that work in your relationship.

- I was angry when we were having that conversation. I'm sorry if that pushed you away.

- "I'm feeling disconnected right now and scared. Could I have a hug?"

- "I don't think we resolved anything there. Let's discuss it again in a different way tomorrow."

- "That was quite an intense discussion for me. Let's sit together and have some tea."

- "You feel distant after that conversation. Is there anything you need?"

- Laugh about something unrelated.

- Talk about something neutral for you both, like gardening or a movie you watched.

Be gentle with each other.

Step 7. Continue the Discussion

If something still needs to be resolved, continue the discussion using the following strategies:

- Agree on when and where is best for the conversation to take place.

- Be curious about how you might stay connected to one another while discussing this issue.

- Practice empathic listening by allowing yourself a moment to stand in their shoes. Listen to understand rather than answer back. Remember that when we listen, we give the other the gift of being understood. It doesn't mean we agree with them.

- Remember they are not the enemy.

If you are in a relationship with a lot of conflict, where there have been betrayals, such as an affair, active addiction, or mental health issues in the relationship, I highly recommend seeking support from a couples' therapist.

Triggers Are Treasures

Triggers can open the door to profound self-healing and help us learn how to stay connected and repair even when things get tricky. The following two chapters explore boundaries and communication, both foundational to cultivating secure relationships and supporting you when triggered.

CHAPTER 9

Boundaries Aren't Just for Other People

Sarah was the oldest of five children. Her father was an alcoholic and sometimes violent. Her mother was completely overwhelmed, so Sarah tried desperately to be a "good girl," to be quiet, and to stay close to her mother. Sarah found it difficult to have boundaries with her mother, who overshared, and found that they would experience similar emotions, finding it difficult to know whose emotions were whose. Sarah grew up with a compulsion to keep the peace and had an anxious attachment adaptation.

Sarah had tried to establish boundaries with her mother many times as an adult but found she would become paralyzed thinking about what her mother would think and feel if she did. The thought of the distance that would be created if she tried to set a boundary made Sarah feel dizzy and panicky in her chest. The idea of appearing mean and being disliked by her mother was intolerable.

Sarah started therapy when she had been dating Edward for about three years. For the entire relationship, Sarah had worried that Edward would leave her. This made it difficult for Sarah to set boundaries with Edward. Things got worse a few months after they moved in together. She found that, although they both worked full time, she would do most of the housework and cooking. She was starting to feel resentful, unappreciated, and burnt-out. Still, she found it almost impossible to say no to Edward and to put any boundaries in place. She would imagine the conversation with Edward ending with him walking out on her, her worst fear.

Having the anxious adaptation, you are likely to have firsthand experience of just how difficult it can be to say no and put a boundary in place in a calm way in your relationship. It might be that anxiety stops you from putting boundaries in place altogether, and you end up feeling burnt-out or resentful or staying in unhealthy relationships for too long. Or you wait too long to put the boundary in place, so when you do, you are so upset, angry, and hurt that it comes out too forcefully and ends up pushing your partner away. This distance is so uncomfortable that you might immediately withdraw the boundary altogether, hoping to move closer again. You might watch yourself do this dance, feel disappointed, and conclude that you are no good at relationships.

Know that you are not alone in this dance and that boundaries can be practiced and embodied. Ultimately, the discomfort of setting boundaries will always be worth the long-term gifts of self-trust, confidence, and healthy relationships.

What Boundaries Are and Why You Need Them

Boundaries are a self-care practice that emerge from a deep knowledge of what is suitable for you. They prevent you from being taken advantage of and protect you from overextending and burning out. They are not fixed; they shift over time and vary from person to person. In a relationship, boundaries help you know what is acceptable behavior and should help both people feel safe. A boundary might sound like, "I'm comfortable kissing in private, but not in public," "I'm glad we follow each other on social media, but I'm not comfortable sharing passwords," or "I'm not comfortable lending you money."

Here are some reasons why you need boundaries:

- To help define who you are, physically, and emotionally

- They are an expression of your values and how you value yourself

- They are part of what differentiates you from other people

- To give a sense of safety and personal space

- They are a way to let others know how to interact with you, what's okay, and what's not

- They are a way to communicate your needs and values

- They enable you to take care of yourself in most situations.

Different Boundary Styles

Boundaries happen developmentally. You learned about boundaries from your experiences and the people around you; this is why we all have different boundary expectations and experiences as adults.

When you were born, you had few boundaries. You were utterly reliant on your primary caregivers and merged with them. You learned about boundaries more as you got older and discovered who you are as separate from your carers and in relation to them. You learned how they responded to your drive to explore the world and shouts of "Me do it!" and "No!" As you grew, your boundary style grew as an adaptation to the environment you were in, much like your attachment style.

There are three styles of boundaries: flexible, porous, and rigid.

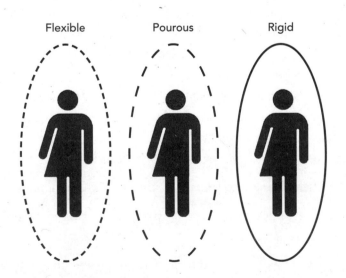

Flexible   Pourous   Rigid

Flexible boundaries

A flexible boundary is like a cell wall that lets some things through but not things that are dangerous or unhealthy for the cell. It is a filtering system that, when functioning well, keeps you safe and energized.

People with flexible boundaries tend to:

- value their own opinions

- be able to live a life aligned with their values

- share personal information appropriately

- be able to say no when they need to and feel okay when others say no to them

- have a strong sense of identity and their personal needs.

A flexible boundary sounds like: "I don't enjoy going to football games with my partner, but I sometimes go because he wants me to, and it's something we can do together."

Porous Boundaries

A porous boundary is like the wall of a cell that has too many holes in it. Because it is too porous, things can get through that might not be healthy. As the filtering system is not working properly, it leaves you feeling unsafe and depleted.

People with porous boundaries tend to:

- have difficulty saying no to others

- people please

- fear rejection

- have the desire to merge with their partner

- put the needs of others before their own

- overshare personal information

- accept bad behavior

- stay in unhealthy relationships for too long

- become burnt-out, depleted, and resentful.

A porous boundary sounds like: "I don't enjoy going to football games with my partner, but I always go because he wants me to, and I don't want to let him down."

Rigid Boundaries

A rigid boundary is like a cell wall that doesn't let much in or out, so it struggles to get the nutrients it needs in and to let go of the toxins it produces. This filtering system often leaves you disconnected from others.

People with rigid boundaries tend to:

- avoid intimacy and vulnerability

- value self-reliance

- have few close relationships

- be protective of personal information

- be detached, even from their partner.

A rigid boundary sounds like: "I don't enjoy going to football games with my partner, so I never go."

We all have a default boundary style, but you might find that you have different boundary styles in different relationships. This is common. I often hear clients say, "I have pretty good boundaries at work, but none at all with my mother. She walks all over me."

Porous Boundaries and the Anxious Adaptation

Porous boundaries and the anxious adaptation go hand in hand. As a child, you learned that you need to modify your behavior to get your need for attachment met, which often meant sacrificing your needs and wants to make everyone else happy. A vivid example of this is given in Jennette McCurdy's (2022) book *I'm Glad My Mom Died*, when she describes being pushed to act and dance as a child to live out her mother's childhood dream of being an actor. When you have porous boundaries, knowing where you end and your partner starts is difficult. There is a tendency to want to merge with your partner and to put their needs ahead of your own, sometimes becoming burnt-out and resentful. The desire to stay connected is so strong that you might allow abusive behavior. The thought of the conflict and relational discomfort that might happen if you say no is not worth it.

What Kind of Boundaries Does Your Family of Origin Have?

We learn about boundaries and relational distance from our family of origin. Explore the intergenerational boundary patterns in your family by answering the questions below in your journal.

- What boundary style do you think your mother had with her mother and father?

- What boundary style do you think your father had with his mother and father?

- What kind of boundary style did your mother have with your father?

- What kind of boundary style did your father have with your mother?

- What kind of boundary style do you have with your parents, now and in the past?

- What kind of boundary style do you have with your current or last partner?

Exploring Your Boundaries

Take a moment to respond to the following prompts in your journal:

- What style of boundaries do you have?

- Do you have the same style in different areas of your life, for example with your mother, father, work, friendships, partnerships, food, and money?

In terms of intimate relationships:

- Do you verbalize the boundaries that you want in your relationship? If yes, give an example. If not, what stops you?

- Do you tend to overexplain your boundaries? What impact do you think overexplaining has on how your boundary is received? Give an example.

- Are you too vague when setting boundaries? If yes, how could you be clearer? Give an example.

- Do you hold people accountable when they overstep a boundary? If yes, give an example. If not, what stops you from keeping the boundary?

Embodied Boundaries

When you have embodied boundaries, you can say no from a place of certainty and inner knowing that the boundary is right for you. You can feel it in your body, and not keeping the boundary would be a form of self-betrayal. You can explain (not overexplain) why you are saying no and hold the boundary, even in the face of pushback. Pushback might be ignoring what you have said, sulking, or being passive aggressive. The other person might try to rationalize their behavior as okay or minimize what is happening and imply that you are overreacting. Pushback aims to test the boundary, which is when you are likely to experience the most discomfort. This discomfort might be:

- fear of being disliked

- fear of seeming ungenerous or mean

- feelings of guilt that arise

- the other person's real or imagined reaction

- not being clear about what your needs are and so struggling to hold the boundary

- not validating your needs (*I need someone else to affirm that I am allowed to have a particular need and boundary*).

Boundaries are multilayered. We have four layers of boundaries:

1. *Physical boundaries.* The first boundary layer is the layer of skin around the body. We explored this in the "Finding Your Edge and Exploring Touch" exercise in chapter 2.

2. *Energetic boundaries.* The second layer is your personal space, a psychological, energetic bubble or container around you. You will sense where your energetic boundary is when people stand too close to you and you feel the urge to step backward.

3. *Internal boundaries.* These are the boundaries you have with yourself, for example, ensuring that you get eight hours or more of sleep per night.

4. *Interpersonal boundaries.* These are the guidelines for interaction in your relationships. They are grounded in beliefs about what you deserve and your ability to communicate it to others.

Finding and Strengthening Your Physical and Energetic Boundaries

When you have an anxious adaptation, boundaries generally need to be strengthened. The first step is to find and embody your physical and energetic boundaries. When you have a strong sense of these boundaries, it becomes easier to discern between what's happening inside you and what's happening with the other person. This leads to a stronger sense of self, and more self-confidence.

Finding Your Embodied Boundary

It would be helpful to have a ball of wool or string about thirty feet long for this exercise and have your journal and pencil at hand.

Maintain a sense of curiosity while doing this exercise. First, you will reawaken the felt sense of your physical boundary, as you did in the "Finding Your Edge and Exploring Touch" exercise in chapter 2. You might do this with a gentle rub, like drying yourself after the shower, which helps you sense your body's outline. You might start at the top of your head and work down to your neck, torso, hips, thighs, knees, ankles, and feet. Do a few complete body movements running your hands from head to toe to get an integrated sense of the fullness of your physical body and boundary.

Now you have located your physical boundary. You will take some time to connect to your energetic boundary. Your energetic boundary is often where you are comfortable with strangers standing. This might be close to the outline of your body, or it might be far away. There are three different ways to explore your embodied boundary:

Option 1. Draw yourself and your boundary on paper. Remember to draw any holes and explore the boundary around the back of your body, above your head, and under your feet. Feel free to use color if that is helpful.

Option 2. Imagine your energetic boundary like a semiporous membrane around your body and explore it from the inside. Use your hands or your imagination to get a sense of this boundary from the inside. See if you can perceive subtle differences in different areas your boundary.

Option 3. Use the colored yarn to draw the boundary around your body on the floor physically. Adjust the yarn to show where it is or cut it to show where there might be holes.

However you decide to explore your boundary, answer these questions and try not to second-guess yourself. Trust what comes. An audio recording of this practice is available online at http://www.psychother-apycentral.health/anxious-attachment.

Now you are connected with your boundary, explore these questions.

- Does your boundary feel closer at the front, back, left, or right of your body, or is it reasonably even the whole way around?

- Is it firm or flimsy? Solid or perforated?

- What images, thoughts, and sensations emerge as you tune in to your energetic boundary? Just notice and take notes in your journal.

- Are there any areas of numbness or openness where you can't sense the boundary at all? Where are these areas?

Strengthening Your Embodied Boundary

When you have grown up with porous boundaries, you need to spend some time strengthening your boundary from the inside and getting to know what a strong, embodied boundary feels like. This practice will help. Take a moment to find the strongest part of your boundary.

- What does it feel like?

- What about it feels stronger?

- As you linger with it, what images come?

- What thoughts emerge?

- What felt sensations are you aware of in your body as you stay with this stronger part of your boundary?

- Does your posture change?

- What would it feel like if your whole boundary was as strong as this part?

- If that was too strong for you, where in your boundary feels just the right level of safety and protection?

- What would it feel like if your whole boundary was like this?

- What might it feel like moving forward with this change in boundary?

- What images, thoughts, and sensations emerge as you imagine this?

- Ask your body and energy body to imprint this new embodied boundary.

Building stronger boundaries happens from the inside out. Take some time to journal about your experience with this practice and make a note to repeat anything that helped you to have a sense of a stronger boundary. When repeated, this exercise helps you stay in touch with your embodied boundary, so when you need to put a limit in place or hold it, it is easier to do.

Internal Boundaries

Internal boundaries are necessary for healthy living. They are little promises to yourself that lead to greater self-respect and self-trust. Having solid and flexible internal boundaries creates a foundation for healthy relationship boundaries.

An internal boundary might be a promise to yourself that you will go to bed at 9:30 p.m. and be asleep by 10:00 p.m. This is good self-care and creates a regular sleep schedule. But, if it is your best friend's birthday on Saturday night, and she is having a party that will finish at 1:00 a.m., it is okay as a one-off to stay up later, knowing that you can sleep in on Sunday. Once or twice a month, it might be okay to be up at 1:00 a.m., but not every night. This is an example of a strong but flexible inner boundary.

Sometimes we don't know where the boundary must be until we cross it and we feel angry with ourselves, disappointed, or ashamed. Writing down our boundaries and carrying them around with us can be helpful as a reminder.

Here is a list of healthy personal boundaries for you to reflect on:

- I will not check work email after _____ (insert time).

- I will not slam doors or shout during arguments. I will take some time out when I need to.

- I will not reconnect with my ex when I feel down.

- I will answer messages when I have the time and space.

- I will stop eating when I feel full.

- I will only think loving thoughts about my body.

- I will get seven to eight hours of sleep per night.

- I will have regular hours of sleep.

- I will take time for self-care every day.

- I will limit my social media intake.

Is there anything you would like to add or remove from this list?

As you think about this list, do you have some inner boundaries you want to establish? Start with small promises, so you set yourself up to win. For example, if you are checking your email until 9:00 p.m., stop at 8:30 p.m. Maybe turn off the internet after 8:30 p.m. so you can't look.

When you have done that for seven days, celebrate. So often, nobody knows about your small wins. If you are like me, you might tend to minimize your successes with something like, *Well, I'm only not reading work email after 8:30 p.m. Most people already do that, so it is not a big deal.* In this one thought, I am invalidating what I have achieved.

This is the moment to step into my nurturing inner parent and say, *Well done, Jen! I'm so proud that you have managed not to check email after 8:30 pm for seven days! I know you were tempted a few times, and it is difficult with everything going on at work. To celebrate, we will take a long bath and listen to your favorite music.*

If you struggle to keep the inner boundary you have set, becoming self-critical will likely lead to feelings of shame. It is much healthier and kinder to meet your struggle with your nurturing parent voice. This might sound like, *Ah, Jen. I noticed you checked your email just before bed at 10:00 p.m. I get why you did that. You were worried that your boss had sent an email, and you are keen to look good at work.* (Note the validation and self-compassion.) *But then it was difficult to switch off, and you laid awake for an hour thinking about work. That's not what we want. I want you to have a full night's sleep. Shall we try again tomorrow, and when the impulse comes to check email, we will do some deep breathing, read our book, or listen to a meditation?*

Take a moment to journal some small inner boundaries you would like to implement.

Interpersonal Boundaries

Healthy boundaries provide a framework for relationships that are mutually loving and respectful. They are essential guidelines for yourself and others about how you like to be treated.

If you often find yourself annoyed by how your partner or a family member treats you, there is likely a boundary issue. Weak boundaries allow:

- people to walk all over you
- people to speak in inappropriate ways in front of you
- people to touch you in ways you are not comfortable with
- people to take advantage of your generosity
- people to expect too much of you physically or emotionally
- people to use guilt to manipulate you.

Notice that all the points above start with "people." When you have weak boundaries, there is often a feeling of these people doing horrible things to you. While you stay in this position, you remain in a situation where life happens to you and you have little agency.

As you realize you deserve to have boundaries, your self-esteem strengthens, and slowly, you start to set boundaries and take the risk of disappointing others. People will likely get upset as you shift your boundaries and get clear on what you will and won't accept in relationships. It is part of the process. Expect it.

Identifying the Boundary You Need

Boundaries help protect you and help you align your life with your values and needs. Knowing your needs can be difficult when you have been taught that your needs are unimportant or should be placed after everyone else's.

In the example at the beginning of this chapter, with Sarah and Edward, Sarah's need is for Edward to take on some of the housework. Before having the conversation, she needs to clarify what she would like Edward to do (what) and why.

What. *"I would like you to cook three days a week and to take ownership of keeping the bathroom clean."* It is good to be specific with the "what," not just "I want you to help out more." Be specific and flexible. Edward might be a terrible cook, so Edward might negotiate to take care of all the cleaning if Sarah takes care of all of the cooking.

Why. *"I'm becoming burnt-out and finding that I am feeling resentful. I want us to have an equal share of household tasks."* The "why" is important because this is where you are validating yourself and clarifying why the boundary is important to you.

Self-validation sounds like this:

- I am allowed to feel angry, confused, or upset about what is happening.

- It is normal to feel _____.

- My feelings are valid even if I can't explain them or they don't make sense to me or someone else.

- I deserve to be loved and cared for.

- I am here to love and care for myself.

- I trust my inner knowing.

- It's okay if nobody agrees with me.

When you have successfully identified the boundary you need and why, when you think about it being adhered to, there will usually be a felt sense of relief.

Take some time to reflect on a current relationship and list what boundaries you need and why you need them. Create a what and why for each boundary.

Supporting Parts of You That Struggle with Boundaries

It is likely that there are parts of you that struggle to set and maintain clear boundaries. These parts need your help to feel safe and supported when setting a boundary. Use this exercise to get to know these parts and give them the support they need. The more they are heard and supported, the easier it is to set boundaries that work for you.

The following steps are explained in more detail in the "Somatic Healing: The Six-Stage Focusing Practice" in chapter 2 (Gendlin 1978).

An audio recording of this practice is available online at http://www.psychotherapycentral.health/anxious-attachment.

Find a quiet space for this practice and make yourself comfortable. When you feel ready, close or lower your eyes.

Step 1. Clearing a Space. Bring your curious, nonjudgmental awareness into your body with openness and kindness, and notice what is present. Bring to mind someone with whom you feel you have porous boundaries. As you imagine this person, notice how your body responds. What sensations arise?

Step 2. Felt Sense. Notice which sensation wants your attention the most right now.

Turn your curiosity toward that sensation to get a fuller sense of it, maintaining some distance between it and you.

Step 3. Handle (Being with the Felt Sense). Focus more deeply on the felt sense with curiosity and kindness, and let any images, memories, thoughts, feeling, or movements come from the felt sense.

Step 4. Resonating (Deep Listening). If it could speak, what would it say? Don't judge or second-guess yourself here. Just go with the first thing that pops into your head, no matter how odd. Make space for what it has said, taking the time to deeply listen, even if you have heard it before. Then check what it said to ensure you have the essence of its message. Is there anything else it would like to share?

Step 5. Asking. *When you are ready, ask it what prevents it from having clearer boundaries with this person. What might it need from you to be supported to have clearer boundaries? Imagine giving it what it is asking for if that is possible.*

Step 6. Receiving. *Receive what came with warmth. Say thank you to the felt sense and your body for all they have shared.*

Gently open your eyes and reorient yourself to the space you are in, and when you are ready, write in your journal what you experienced and what your felt sense had to share. You may like to repeat this exercise a few times to allow different parts to speak that may be holding fear and uncertainty when setting boundaries.

Strengthening Porous Boundaries with Others

Now that the parts of you holding concern about setting boundaries have been supported, let's explore what it might feel like to have stronger boundaries with the person you thought about in the exercise above. A guided audio recording of this exercise is available at http://www.psychotherapycentral.health/anxious-attachment.

- Bring to your awareness the person with whom you have porous boundaries and worked with in the exercise "Supporting Parts of You That Struggle with Boundaries."

- Bring to mind a boundary that you would like to have with this person.

- What would it feel like in your body to have this boundary firmly in place?

- Linger here for a time and notice what thoughts or feelings emerge as you hold this boundary.

- Notice if there is a change in posture as you imagine holding this boundary. How do you hold your head? What happens to your spine and your shoulders?

- Experiment with standing up and imagine holding this boundary lovingly and firmly and then notice how your legs feel.

- What does your future look like with this boundary clearly in place?

Take some time to journal your experience with this exercise.

Because boundaries were so daunting for Sarah, she did the practices in this chapter for a few weeks before communicating her new boundaries to Edward. When she talked to Edward about the split of housework, she was shocked to feel somehow sure about her request. She was still aware of a slight panic in her chest about how he might respond, but it did not overtake the conversation as it had done in the past. She felt grounded and embodied and could deal with his response. It was a completely new feeling for Sarah. When Edward responded to the request for more help, he agreed that Sarah had been doing most of the work and that he'd been feeling tired and appreciated it, but that it was time for him to contribute more. To her amazement, he agreed with all of her requests. Sarah realized that before she learned about boundaries, she had been passively hinting to Edward in the hope of him knowing what was wrong. Being direct, having a clear what and why, and being embodied changed everything.

Embodied Boundaries Create Safety

In this chapter, you identified the boundaries you need and worked on embodying your physical, energetic, internal, and interpersonal boundaries. You have rebuilt them from the ground up. The next chapter will break down how to communicate your boundaries to your partner and family, even when feeling anxious.

CHAPTER 10

Communicate Through Your Anxiety

You have probably had the experience of knowing you need to say something, but feeling anxious about how it will be received, like Sarah from the prior chapter. The thought of the other person's reaction fills you with panic and dread. You might find that your mind goes completely blank in the moment, preventing you from speaking at all, or that lots of words and emotions come flooding out that are confusing or frightening for your partner. You would rather continue as you are, drop hints, and hope the other person changes their behavior, which often leads to resentment and anger when they don't hear your hints or take your requests seriously. The resentment builds until you explode, with all the energy directed at the other person and little awareness of your responsibility for allowing the situation to continue. By the time your need is shared, the pain is so great and the need to be connected so strong that a deep cry comes straight from the attachment wound that asks, "Where is my person? Am I safe?"

The other form of communication you may have used is passive aggressive. This is when you are angry about something, but don't share it with your partner directly. Instead, you share the anger indirectly by sulking, giving them the silent treatment, using sarcasm, and denying your true feelings, like saying you are fine when you are not. When you have met your needs using one of these styles, you have likely been left feeling that you have somehow let yourself down.

When you have the anxious adaptation, you have often experienced inconsistency and not much exposure to the modeling of clear, assertive communication. Communication is critical in cultivating secure relationships. Communication is the manifestation of the flow of energy between you as a couple. You might find that you become triggered and loud in arguments, but your intention is not to hurt your partner. Rather you are feeling unheard, unappreciated, and fearful. The good news is that you can work toward clearer, more authentic, assertive communication that is also more vulnerable and brings greater confidence, self-trust, and intimacy.

The Basics of Communication

As communication is a flow, it is important to learn how to give first. Giving in communication is done through empathic listening and validation. Secondly, you learn how to express yourself effectively and vulnerably by being in touch with your core emotions and attachment needs.

Empathic Listening

Think of communication as a dance in the space between you and your partner. When you communicate, you are doing it with your tone of voice, posture, eye contact, and spoken words. When we think about communication, we usually think about the message we want to convey to the other person. This is the first mistake. The first step toward successful communication is empathic listening.

In the empathic listening space, you are connected to your heart and safely anchored in social engagement. You are genuinely curious about the other person's experience as a fellow human being you care for. Empathic listening says, "I am here for you." It is the practice of bringing your whole presence into the moment to fully listen with love (Nhat Hahn 2013). Empathic listening doesn't sound very exciting, but it is one of the most potent ways to build strong relationships and secure attachment when done with your whole heart.

Listening empathically involves:

- becoming receptive and putting aside your point of view for a moment

- letting go of your defenses

- trying your best to understand the other person's experience without it having to make sense to you or you having to agree with what they are saying.

Empathic listening is difficult when we feel (or are) accused of something. We tend to become defensive. It takes a great deal of maturity and strength to listen through the accusation, find the point of pain they are trying to communicate, and imagine how that might feel for them.

Following are examples of a defensive response and an empathic response to an accusation:

Accusation: *You said you would call me when you were away, and I didn't hear a thing, not even a text.*

Defensive response: *Sorry, but I don't remember saying I would call you, and I was in a meeting until 10:00 p.m. I was exhausted. I was only gone for one night. Is it such a big deal? I'm here now.*

Empathic response: *I'm so sorry, you are right. I could have sent a text. I imagine not texting or calling made you feel forgotten and maybe unloved. That wasn't my intention.*

Notice in this empathic response, the listener is trying to identify the attachment needs: to feel important and loved. It doesn't matter if you guess the attachment needs incorrectly. Your partner will usually correct you.

Validation

The second magic ingredient for effective, heart-centered communication is validation. Validation is simply agreeing that a feeling exists. Because you have experienced invalidation as a child, receiving validation as an anxiously attached person is profoundly healing. As a child, you were likely told you were overreacting, there was nothing to be upset about, you were causing a scene, or your sibling didn't behave like that, so why did you? The implication was that there was something inherently wrong with you and nothing wrong with the situation you found yourself in or the behavior of the people around you. As a child, you assumed they were correct, that you were flawed, and that your emotions were too much and somehow wrong. Having your feelings validated and understood as an adult is a corrective experience; this is why validation is so powerful for you—both self-validation and validation from others.

SELF-VALIDATION

Self-validation comes when you understand your current emotional reaction in the context of your history and accept it as valid. It is essentially permitting yourself to experience a feeling. When you remember that feelings are messengers, this is easier.

Here is what invalidation sounds like: "I don't understand why I feel so devastated that he canceled our date on Sunday. Most people don't react this way. There's something wrong with me."

Here's what self-validation sounds like: "It makes sense that I'm sad and disappointed that he canceled our date. The pain reminds me of all the times dad was supposed to have me for the day and just didn't show up. I remember how let down I used to feel. Nothing is wrong with me. My feelings make sense given my childhood experiences."

This is an example of being triggered. Unprocessed pain from the past is felt in a present-day situation. Validating your emotional experience and turning toward yourself rather than becoming critical is vital here. This would be the perfect cue to take some time to talk to your inner child, as you learned in chapter 4.

VALIDATION IN RELATIONSHIPS

When validating your partner, it is important to remember that you do not have to agree with how the feeling came about. Simply to give them permission to have the feeling. Validation is more powerful when we can take a moment to imagine what their experience might be like and to have empathy. When you genuinely empathize with your partner, they will feel it.

Invalidation is when you ignore, minimize, or judge someone else's emotional experience. Invalidation sounds like: "You shouldn't be so upset. I can't control who texts me and at what time. You're being unreasonable." "I don't know why we are still discussing this. It happened six months ago. Surely you should be over it by now?"

Validation sounds like: "I know what it's like to feel second best, it's terrible, and it wasn't my intention for you to feel that way. I can hear how upset you still are about what happened. I get it. It must be really hard."

Here is an example of how to validate your partner when you disagree with them.

Issue: My partner is upset because my mother says she is not religious enough.

Invalidation sounds like: *Ignore what she said. It's not a big deal. I don't know why you are so upset about this.*

Validation sounds like: *I can see this is a big deal to you. I imagine it hurts to feel that you are not enough somehow. Like you are being criticized. I'm guessing you were hoping to be close to my mother, and this feels like a block to that dream. Am I right?*

Having the capacity to hear and validate each other's emotional experience is a powerful tool in any relationship. For someone with the anxious adaptation, it has the power to aid in the healing of the original attachment wound. Deep intimacy, safety, and connectedness are the result when you are permitted to take up space and your partner doesn't retreat from your emotions. Instead, you are deeply heard and held. It is one of the most potent aphrodisiacs I know.

How to Deal with Invalidation

You probably find when your emotions or the issue you are talking about is being invalidated or minimized, you are triggered. This is common because an old wound is being reopened. There is part of you that remembers this experience and reacts as a younger part. The keys to dealing with invalidation are self-validation and communication with your partner.

Invalidation sounds like: *You knew I was going out for Pete's birthday and that I'd be home late. I don't know why you are so upset.*

Self-validation sounds like: *It makes sense I'm feeling panicky because Pete is a wild card, and I don't trust them when they are together. I needed him to be home earlier and to send me a few texts through the night to feel safe.*

· Communicating with your partner: "I can sense you being defensive right now, and that makes sense because you feel attacked. Is that right? What I'm really trying to say is that I feel scared when you go out with Pete because he's a wild card. I would feel safer if you could keep in touch with me by sending me a few texts through the night, and maybe we could agree on an appropriate time boundary, say 1:00 a.m?"

Five Steps to Clear and Vulnerable Communication

When you have learned that your needs are not important and, in some cases, that the needs of the parent are bigger and more important than your needs, identifying and communicating them to your partner can feel overwhelming. Learning to communicate your needs and boundaries is like anything else you learn for the first time: it takes time and practice. But the payoff is worth it. When you can communicate your needs and boundaries effectively, you increase the level of safety you feel internally because you know that you will stand up for yourself and your self-respect increases.

You are the only expert on you. Nobody else can read your mind and know what you need in all the areas of relationship. It is up to you to first identify your needs and then let your partner know. Once you have communicated your needs, there is no obligation for your partner to fill them. But it is important there is space in the relationship for both of your needs to be heard, which can be a deeply healing experience. Here are five steps for clear communication.

Step 1. What Happened

This is factual and observed and does not include feelings or assumptions. "*I noticed* when I was talking about my issue at work you started to read messages on your phone."

Step 2. Empathy: What I Imagine Was Happening for You

This is where you take a moment to step into your partner's world and imagine what might be going on for them. This is empathy in action. It has the effect of broadening your perspective and making them feel understood. It builds connection and creates a softening in the communication. "*I imagine* a lot is happening at work and that you feel anxious to stay on top of things."

Step 3. Core Emotion

This is the deeper feeling, often hidden under the emotion you instinctively want to express. Focus on the core emotion when communicating. "*I felt* sad (rejected, alone, and let down)."

Step 4. Attachment Needs

This is the flavor of the connection you yearn for with your partner, the attachment need. When communicating, it is important to express your attachment needs, which often involves some vulnerability.

As a reminder, here is a list of attachment needs:

- to be understood and accepted

- to feel loved, wanted, and important to your partner

- to know your partner will be there when you need them

- to feel close to your partner, like the two of you are a team

- to feel appreciated.

"I need to feel like we are a team, that I'm important to you and can rely on you."

Step 5. Clear Request

This is a clearly defined request, not abstract or vague, and respects your partner. Rather than express what you *don't* want, say what you *do* want. Make it a clear action. A vague request would be to say, "I'd like you to pay more attention to me." There is no guidance on exactly how to give you more attention. A clear request sounds like: *"Would you be willing to give me your full attention to talk about this issue for ten minutes?"*

Holding relational tension is difficult when you have an anxious adaptation. You tend to want to resolve everything immediately. You may need to go for a walk, call a friend, or use another resource to hold yourself until your partner feels that they are in a place to debrief with you. This ensures that your request is a request and not a demand.

Notice the difference between, "I'm talking about what's happening at work, and you're more interested in your phone!" and "*I noticed* when I was talking about my issue at work, you started to read messages on your phone. *I imagine* you have a lot going on at work too that you need to keep track of. *I felt* sad and hurt. *I need* to feel like we are a team, that I'm important to you and I can rely on you. *Would you be willing* to give me your full attention to discuss this issue for ten minutes?"

Here is a helpful formula that you can use when you need to communicate a need (Rosenburg 2015):

I noticed _____.

I imagine _____.

I felt _____.

I need _____.

Would you be willing _____?

Vulnerability, Your Core Emotions, and Attachment Needs

You have probably found from your work in chapter 7 that identifying your core emotion and attachment need in a situation makes you feel vulnerable. When you connect with these things, there is usually a pull at your heart and often tears as you admit them to yourself. They are painful because they have gone unmet and sometimes unacknowledged for so long.

When you are in a relationship and want to build intimacy, vulnerability is part of that process. As you become more vulnerable, holding on to your heart and testing the waters a bit at a time is important. Healthy trust is formed a little bit at a time, and small consistencies compound to form a solid foundation of trust. For example, your partner turns up when they say they will, they keep confidences you have shared privately, and they are ready to commit to a long-term relationship.

Practicing the Five Steps of Clear Communication

Journaling is a powerful tool to help you clarify your needs and boundaries and how to communicate them. It can be like chatting with a supportive friend.

It might look like: "When I got angry at Rob about going away for work, I shot a three-second cutting comment his way. In couples therapy, he said that he thought about that comment all day, and it made him feel unnerved and off-kilter for the day. I had no idea. Most of the time, I think he hears what I say and then feels angry with me and pulls away, or he forgets because it doesn't make sense to him. Either way, I feel the distance and sad that he doesn't care more. Caring would look like him asking me questions about the comment and being

curious to understand why I'm angry. I realize I'm misreading his emotional responses and need him to tell me how he feels. That would also
make me feel safer and much closer to him."

First, work the five steps in your journal. A blank version of this
table is available online at http://www.psychotherapycentral.health
/anxious-attachment.

1	What happened (factual and observed)	I noticed I snapped at you.
2	Empathy	I imagine I was pretty scary, and you wanted to get away or didn't know how to respond in the moment, and so you withdrew.
3	Core emotions	I felt sad.
4	Attachment needs	I need to feel loved, like I'm important to you, and safe together.
5	Clear request	Would you be willing to tell me how you are impacted when I snap at you?

Then, write out the script for communicating the needs and boundaries you identified above. For example, "I have realized that I find it
difficult to know how you are feeling sometimes. When I snapped at
you the other day, I thought you were angry or uninterested because
you didn't talk about it with me. I imagine I was pretty scary when I
snapped, and you just wanted to get away or maybe didn't know how
to respond in the moment, so you withdraw. I felt sad and angry that
we couldn't communicate better. It was a surprise to hear that you
were feeling off-kilter all day. I know it might be difficult, but I think it
would make me feel closer to you and safer if you could have told me
how that conversation was impacting you. Something like, 'Hey Rach, I
just want to let you know that I'm feeling a bit unresolved and unsure
about what happened this morning. I'm hoping we can talk about it
more later today' would be enough."

Your turn. Think of a time when you felt triggered or upset recently and work through the five steps.

1	What happened (factual and observed)	I noticed …
2	Empathy	I imagine …
3	Core emotions	I felt …
4	Attachment needs	I need *to* …
5	Clear request	Would you be willing *to* …

Being Assertive

Assertiveness is when we have strong self-esteem and maintain healthy boundaries. Assertive communication is direct and clear and makes space for the other person. When we are assertive, we tend to experience less anxiety and depression because we can stand in our truth while attempting to understand how the other person feels about what is being discussed. Assertiveness brings with it a greater sense of agency.

The first step in being assertive is to know your needs. If you are uncertain about your needs, then it makes sense that those around you will also be uncertain about what you need. You will find it difficult to communicate your needs, and you will not be taken seriously when you do.

For example, your sister wants you to lend her money. You say no but worry when she becomes more withdrawn than usual. Without a conversation, you change your mind and lend her the money. A few weeks later, she has still not repaid you, and asks to borrow more. You find yourself feeling taken advantage of and start to feel angry.

Being assertive in this relationship might sound like, "We agreed that you would repay the amount you borrowed last time, but you haven't repaid me yet. I imagine you are struggling with your work situation, and I feel for you. I feel sad about this, but I have to be honest, I'm uncomfortable lending you more money without first being repaid. I value our relationship, and I don't want money to come between us."

When you are assertive, you don't play games. Below are some situations, old communication styles of game playing, and ways to communicate clearly and assertively to help get your needs met.

Situation: You talk to your partner; they're not really listening. You feel disrespected and unimportant.

Game playing: You stop midsentence and storm off, expecting them to come after you and apologize.

Clear communication: You share that you value their input in your life, "Would you be willing to put your phone down for five minutes and hear me?"

Situation: You find out through social media that your partner was out without you on Saturday night and feel hurt and rejected.

Game playing: You post pictures of yourself with your ex on social media and don't answer his calls.

Clear communication: "When you don't let me know what you are doing on the weekend, I feel disappointed and agitated because I need a sense of safety in our relationship. I'm wondering if, in the future, you could let me know what you are up to on the weekend, even if they are last-minute plans?"

The next time your partner goes out on the weekend, they may not let you know. Clear communication doesn't mean that suddenly all of your requests will be met, but it does mean that you are clear about your needs and have spoken your truth. If your partner doesn't do what you have clearly asked for, you can get curious about that together to explore what happened for your partner and for you. You can go back to chapter 7 and review "Tracking a Negative Cycle."

Learning to communicate clearly and break the habit of game playing allows us to be clear with our needs and will quickly let us know if we are in the right relationship or not.

Here are some things that block assertive communication:

- You think you will be judged or rejected.

- You assume the other person will be upset.

- You doubt the validity of your needs.

- You avoid potentially uncomfortable situations and conflict.

- You lack the skills to communicate assertively.

There are many reasons people avoid being assertive. I find the two biggest reasons are they fear the other person's response (conflict avoidance) and they don't know how to be assertive. When they don't know how, it is often because they have not had it modeled to them. This is where the exercises in this chapter will help.

Embodied Communication

I had very little assertive communication modeled to me growing up. Most of the communication was done in a passive-aggressive manner, and when the person holding in all the anger couldn't do it anymore, there were explosions. As an adult, I tried being passive aggressive in one of my relationships, but the other person didn't respond. I then figured out that I was hoping he would guess what was wrong with me and do what I wanted him to do. I was expecting him to mind read. When I realized this expectation was a bit silly, I reverted to assertive communication, and low and behold, I started to get my needs met.

The most significant step in my leap from sulky and passive aggressive to assertive communication came from my time alone practicing. I would journal my needs and boundaries and write a script to get all the elements clear, as in the "Practicing the Five Steps of Clear Communication" exercise in this chapter. I would then imagine the person in front of me and start to read the script aloud.

The first time I did this, I remember stumbling over words, having to repeat myself, and stopping to cough multiple times. My body was totally uncomfortable with this new style of communication. Before this experience, I had thought of myself as quite confident and a fairly good communicator. This made me aware of just how difficult it was for me to have highly charged, intimate, and vulnerable conversations. I sucked!

When you are not used to assertive communication, you need to practice. There is no way around this. It is vital that you read the script aloud. Practicing will allow your body to align with the words you want to say and for you to communicate with the energy you intend.

Embodied Communication

Here is a seven-step process for embodied communication that draws on all the skills you have learned so far in this book. Remember it will probably be awkward at first, but once you become more familiar with this style of communication, it will become much easier.

Step 1. Journal. Journal your needs and boundaries, ensuring what you are requesting honors the other person too.

Step 2. Write a script. Write a script of how you would like to communicate it using the five steps. See the "Practicing the Five Steps of Clear Communication" exercise above.

Step 3. Find out what your inner child needs. Check in with your inner child, as you learned in chapter 4. Ask them how they feel about the conversation and what they might need as you have it. For example, my child likes to hide inside my heart while I have difficult conversations.

Step 4. Pay attention to the sensations in your body. In a quiet place, take the time to read the script aloud. As you are reading, notice what is going on in your body. If intense sensations arise, take a moment to be with them in a felt sense way, as in chapter 2, "Somatic Healing: The Six-Stage Focusing Practice." When you do this, you are using current situations as an avenue for healing.

Step 5. Embody your script. Read and reread your script until there is flow in the words and your body feels more aligned with what you are saying. It might take a few sessions for this feeling to come, and that's fine. The aim is not to memorize the words but to imbibe the felt experience of aligning with them. Once you have aligned with the energy of what you want to say, the words come more easily.

Step 6. Have the conversation. At an appropriate time, preferably in a relaxed environment, have the conversation. If there is resistance, try to empathize with it and understand it rather than become defensive. Be open to the possibility of an outcome that suits you both that you have not yet considered.

Step 7. Congratulate yourself. No matter the outcome, congratulate yourself for practicing. The more you practice, the easier it will be. You will find the words more effortless, and stay calmer for longer. Be gentle with yourself in the process. This is a big part of your healing and empowerment journey.

Communicating When Triggered

A major challenge for the anxious adaptation is how a conversation starts when triggered. Your nervous system has sensed danger and sent you into a fight-or-flight nervous system response. This is great if you are running from danger, but it can be problematic if you would like to have an effective conversation with your partner.

If you are triggered, the first step in clear communication is to notice that you are activated and to use a resource from the "Triggers and Resources" exercise from chapter 6 to help bring your nervous system into ventral vagal (social engagement) or as close as you can get to it. Be gentle with yourself here. Your nervous system is learning how to regulate, just like you. Try a few different resources and track your nervous system as you learned to do in the "Tracking Your Nervous System: Regulation in Practice" exercise in chapter 6. When you feel less activated, do some journaling about what happened and what your needs and boundaries might be.

When Fear Blocks Communication

The biggest block to communication is often your imagined reaction of the other person and the space between you that will result. Sometimes the imagined response is accurate, and sometimes not. You can't control the other person's reaction.

Here is a process to try if you feel anxious about communicating your needs with your partner.

When Fear Blocks Communication

When you think about communicating something and have a strong reaction to the thought of it, you can be sure that a part of you is scared. It is often a younger part of you who is scared of being abandoned or separated from the person they love. In this process, you will learn how to meet that part of yourself, validate its experiences and fears, and attune to its needs. When that part of you feels safe, you'll find that much of the fear will disappear. An audio recording of this practice is available online at http://www.psychotherapycentral.health /anxious-attachment.

> Sitting quietly, gently intend to let go of anything that has been bothering you, perhaps placing it to the side to return to later. Begin to notice your breathing, in and out. Allow the breath to guide you inward.

> Gently invite the part of you feeling anxious about communicating to come forward. Welcome that part and let them know you are glad to see them. Ask that part how they are doing and how they are feeling about having this difficult conversation.

> If they are feeling scared or worried, validate those feelings. It makes sense that this part would feel nervous or apprehensive, maybe they are afraid of being abandoned, getting into an argument, or letting people down. Make space for whatever feelings arise; they are all valid.

Let them know that you are there for them and that they will not have to do the talking. Let them know that you are an adult and will take care of this. If they like, they can stand behind you or hide in your heart while you have this difficult conversation.

They might not trust that you can have this conversation. Trust is something that builds over time. Let them know that you are learning and growing and will do your very best to communicate effectively, and if it's not perfect, that's okay. Your best is good enough.

Before you leave, ask if they need anything else from you. If there is and it is reasonable, commit to doing it with or for them when possible.

Thank that part of you for coming forward today. Allow that part to shrink to about two inches high and step inside your heart.

Take a deep breath and become aware of your body again. Moving your hands and feet, thank yourself for this memorable experience.

Take some time to journal your experiences with this exercise.

Communication That Is Fertilizer for Your Relationship

The following types of communication can be fertilizer for everyone, regardless of attachment style:

- Anything that is genuine and helps your partner feel seen, heard, understood, and loved

- Empathic listening

- Validation

- Noticing what's working, for example, "I felt so loved when you…"

If you have the anxious adaptation, the following are fertilizer for you:

- Emotional validation, self-validation, and validation from others

- Resisting the urge to blame, criticize, and express anger, which causes defensiveness and blocks communication

- Being curious about what is happening for *both* of you

- Avoiding the tendency to look out for negative things in the relationship, practicing appreciating the small stuff, and learning to look for the positive things in your relationship and partner

- Taking the time to connect with your core emotion and attachment needs in any situation

- Getting clear on what you need and asking for it with a clear request

- Resisting the urge to play games or engage in protest behaviors, like sulking, threatening, or demanding

- Understanding that when your partner withdraws, they are often trying to protect the relationship

- Helping your partner feel appreciated

- Resisting the pressure to resolve everything right away during a conflict in case your partner might need more time than you to process what happened.

If you have the avoidant adaptation and are in a relationship with someone with the anxious adaptation, the following aspects of communication are profoundly healing:

- Resisting the urge to pull away when your partner expresses anger

- Understanding that protest behaviors from your anxious partner are a call for connection

- Learning to identify and communicate your feelings, although it often feels overwhelming and scary

- Trying your best to connect emotionally through empathic listening rather than getting logical and problem-solving

- Avoiding dismissing or minimizing things that are important to your partner, even if you don't understand or agree

- If you feel yourself shutting down, not feeling anything, or withdrawing, letting your partner know that you are shutting down and struggling to stay connected

- When you feel discomfort, trying to stay in touch with the sensations and feelings in your body

- During conflict, allowing yourself the space to process what is happening and taking a break if you need one and then going back to your partner and finish the discussion to prevent avoidance.

Communication Increases Intimacy

Well done! Learning to communicate differently changed my life, and it will change yours too. I became a lot less scary and was able to let the people I love know how I felt before it exploded out of me. To my surprise, I found that vulnerable communication actually increased the level of intimacy in my relationship. Rather than being rejected, I was heard and my needs taken into more account by me and my partner. Take your time with this chapter. Read it and reread it. Vulnerable communication takes practice.

Now you have spent a lot of time with your inner world and exploring your intimate relationships. It is time to explore your connection to the world in the next chapter.

CHAPTER 11

Meaningful Connections in the World Abound

Let's pause momentarily and acknowledge how far you have come while journeying through this book. There has already been a substantial amount of discovery, healing, and growth. In chapters 1 through 5, you anchored your connection to self. In chapters 6 through 10, you explored securely attaching to others, and in this chapter, you will do the vital work of reconnecting to nature, spirit, and meaning.

In our relatively recent human history, as hunter-gatherers, our survival depended on being connected with other humans and nature. Hunter-gatherer groups that still exist today prioritize sharing, reciprocity, and connection (Narvaez 2019). Connection is valued and vital to survival. Although we seem more connected than ever before, many people are experiencing unprecedented levels of loneliness and disconnection (Jeste, Lee, and Cacioppo 2020). Disconnection is at the core of the anxious adaptation. This is why the healing process is one of reconnection.

Exploring Your Connection to Nature

In my clinic, over the years, I have noticed that most people with the anxious adaptation lack a meaningful connection to nature. Many desire to have it but live in big cities and have busy lives, which limits their interaction with and connectedness to nature. I find when working with these individuals, even imagining a natural place and connecting with the energy of that place has the effect of calming the nervous system, helping them feel more grounded, safer, and more peaceful. There is something about connecting with nature that gives people a more profound sense of self. After connecting deeply with a place in nature, common responses are:

"I feel more alive, like the edge between me and the forest has become blurred, and I am part of the forest. It is deeply reassuring. I get a sense of the forest holding me and helping me."

"I am left with a sense of deep connectedness with life that gives personal meaning and a sense of belonging" (Boelhouwers 2013, 18).

"Everything around me was supporting me…. Everything I needed was there" (Grafanaki 2013, 90).

"I have so much support that I can be with every part of me, accept it, love it, and support it in whatever way it needs me to" (Abraham 2013, 2).

This is unsurprising, as much research has demonstrated the benefits of connecting with nature. These include coping with changing environments and an increased connection with self, agency, self-esteem, and sense of belonging, as well as reduced anxiety and stress, blood pressure, cortisol levels, and headaches (Berger 2006, 2008; Fuller et al. 2007; McLeod 2013; Gelsthorpe 2017).

For the first time in human history, many people have little connection with nature or spirit (Roszak 2001; Gelsthorpe 2017). Is the result of this disconnection varying forms of anxiety and depression?

Journaling Your Connection to Nature

Memories of being in nature can have a powerful calming effect. Take some time to reflect on a recent experience you had in nature.

- When was the last time you were in nature and felt present with the nature around you?

- What do you remember about that experience?

- Do you have a special place in nature where you feel relaxed and safe?

- What is it about that place that draws you there?

- How does your body feel as you remember the sounds, smells, and felt experience of that place?

Connecting to Nature

The following exercise needs to be done in nature. You could find a quiet place in your local park or, better yet, go to a forest. A forest is best because the air is full of phytoncides, wood essential oils, which are chemicals that improve human immune function (Li 2010). This exercise aims to explore your relationship with nature, where nature is your partner, and has its foundation in both Forest Bathing and Focusing (Clifford 2021; Gendlin 1964). In this practice, you explore "what it means to be part of the web of relatedness connecting all living beings" (Clifford 2021, 42).

Step 1. Awareness Through the Senses

Follow your body. Walk through the forest slowly, with awareness. Notice the differences in the trees and certain areas of the forest. Notice how your body responds as you walk through different areas and which places your body feels drawn to. Follow the signals from your body and your curiosity. When the place feels right in your body, find somewhere to sit for at least ten minutes. Be still as you sit. What do you notice? How does it feel in your body to be in this place in the forest?

See. You might start by becoming aware of your surroundings, noticing exactly what you can see. Notice where your eyes are drawn and allow your eyes to be an interface between you and the nature around you. Take a moment to notice the large shapes of the forest as well as the details of things close to you. Do you see any patterns or notice how different plants or trees seem to meet each other?

Hear. Become aware of what you can hear. Notice the louder noises and the softer sounds. Are there any rhythms in what you can hear? Do any of the sounds form layers of sounds around you? How do they interconnect?

Touch. Notice how the earth is supporting you where you are sitting. What is it like to feel the earth holding you? How do your clothes feel on your body? Can you feel a breeze on your skin? What temperature is it? How does your body respond to the sense of being touched by nature?

Smell. Notice what you can smell in your space. What are the more pungent smells, and what are the scents that live under those that are more subtle? As these smells enter your nose, how do they travel through your body, and how does your body respond to them? How would it feel to breathe this air deeply into your body?

Step 2. Explore Your Connection with the Aliveness of Nature

Now you have slowed down and connected with the forest in a meaningful way, you can explore the three practices below, which will deepen your connection.

Tree roots. Find a tree that appears healthy and attracts you and approach it. Introduce yourself through your heart. Take a moment to marvel at its wonder and magnificence. Become aware of the interchange between you and the tree. Know that its tree roots are supporting you. Most roots expand underground four times the circumference of the tree canopy. What does it feel like in your body to be supported by the trees around you? What would it feel like to be this tree? To have such a firm and thick trunk and your branches reaching so far into the air? What would it feel like to have the same powerful roots submerged into the soil, absorbing nutrients and supporting the forest floor? How does the tree's interconnectedness with the forest impact you? How does your body respond to this tree and its interconnectedness?

The breath. Sitting in a comfortable place, turn your awareness to your breath. Notice the sensation of the air moving into your body through your nostrils. Notice how the air feels as it enters your lungs and belly. What scents are in the air? If there was a color to the air, what would it be? Now place your hands on your stomach and bring the air down into the abdomen so you feel it open in all directions. You may need to contract the stomach a little on the exhale. You are taking the air deeply into your body. Become aware that as you inhale, you accept the gift of oxygen the trees produce, which takes in the carbon dioxide you produce. Through the air, you are connected to everything. Continue this breathing for at least five minutes.

The healing breath. Take some of the breath from the above practice to different parts of your body, especially any areas that feel depleted or hold pain. Simply breathe in and imagine the breath going to that part of your body, nourishing and supporting it. Imagine that area receiving whatever it might need. You might feel heavy energy leaving certain areas of your body to be replaced by this fresh, vital forest energy. Allow yourself to follow your breath and your body's inner wisdom in connection with the forest.

Connecting with What Is Meaningful

Research has shown that focusing on extrinsic goals where we value praise, reward, money, appearance, and social recognition reduces well-being, vitality, and self-actualization, and increases depression and anxiety (Kasser and Ryan 1996; Kasser and Ahuvia 2002). The same research has demonstrated that intrinsic goals, such as self-acceptance, creating a sense of community, and improving health, bring about less depression and increased well-being and self-actualization.

Connecting with What Is Meaningful

Take some time to journal and reflect on these questions (Kasser and Ryan 1996).

- How important is it to you that you are (rate each with a score of 1 to 10, with 10 being very important to you):

    a. physically attractive to others

    b. have expensive things

    c. are well-known

    d. earn a lot of money

    e. have status

    f. have the ideal body?

    These are all extrinsic factors.

- How important is it that you are (rate each from 1 to 10, with 10 being very important to you.):

    a. healthy

    b. do meaningful work

    c. contribute to your community

    d. have deep friendships

    e. have life energy

    f. help others?

    These are all intrinsic factors.

- What have been the three most meaningful experiences in your life so far?

- What was it about each incident that made it meaningful? For example: *The birth of my children: creating, being pushed to the edge, an act of love, awe in nature.*

- How can you have more experiences that hold meaning for you? You might be unable to repeat the experience, such as having another child. Still, you might be able to think of things involving the elements that made it meaningful, like creativity and finding awe in nature.

Connecting to the Stronger Part of Self

We began this journey connecting to self and will end it connecting to the stronger part of you. You might call this stronger part your spirit, soul, or Higher Self. Most anxious parts of self, when met with the energy of compassion, curiosity, and enduring love, will feel calmed and reassured. Having a connection with this part of self has been life-changing for me and for many of my clients.

Connecting to the Stronger Part of Self

An audio recording of this practice is available online at http://www.psychotherapycentral.health/anxious-attachment.

> *Find a comfortable place to lie or sit down where you can relax deeply. When you are ready, close your eyes, take a deep breath, and gift this time to yourself. Take another deep breath and let go of anything that is distracting you. You might like to gently place it to your side, knowing you can return to it after this meditation.*
>
> *Gently bring your attention to your breath. Notice your chest moving up and down.*
>
> *If you find thoughts coming up, notice them, and let them float away. Remember that you are not your thoughts, and gently return your focus to your breath.*
>
> *Allow yourself to start to feel relaxed, allow all tension to drain from your head, let your neck and torso relax and become heavy, allow all tension to release from your arms and legs, and replace it with a deep sense of relaxation and peace. Allow your whole body to be relaxed as you begin to connect with the core of you.*
>
> *You will now ask to connect with a "stronger part" of yourself. You might think of this part as your observer self, Higher Self, soul, or spirit. It is the part of you that can witness yourself with love and compassion. It is the indestructible, eternal part*

of you. Be open and curious about what that part might look or feel like.

This part has helped you survive everything that you have gone through. It has been with you, holding and supporting you. Invite that part to take up more space and grow stronger as you focus on it. How does it feel to allow this part to step forward more? How does it feel in your body? In your mind? In your heart?

Focus on the heart area and notice any sensations there. Allow your heart to fill with light. Take a moment to remember all the people in your life who you love. Remember times in your life when you felt loved.

Now, see yourself standing in front of your heart as you are now and as a child, and shower yourself and your child with your love. You might see this love as a particular color as the two of you are saturated in it. Breathe it in until you both feel full. Know that you both deserve your love.

Take a moment to reflect on the values that create a meaningful life for you. What would your life look like if you were aligned with meaningful work, connections, and deep friendships, and were contributing to society?

What are you doing and feeling in this vision? Who's with you? What are they doing and feeling? What can you see happening? What sounds can you hear? What sensations can you feel in your body? How does your posture change? Know that you deserve to have a life filled with meaning and joy. Take your time and linger here for as long as you would like; you could even pause this recording.

Thank yourself for taking this time to create a vision of what could be. For opening the door to something different, thank your spirit and heart for their continued presence.

Start to become aware of your body, the feeling of your feet on the floor, your weight on the chair. Gently stretch your body as it would like to move. When you feel ready, open your eyes and take in your surroundings. Allow yourself the time you need to land fully back in your space.

Take some time to journal your experience with this meditation.

You Are Enough

Take a moment to flip through your journal and see just how much learning, discovering, and growing you have done since committing to the journey of this book. Has something created a significant shift for you, or have there been many little gems along the way?

You have probably found as you have worked through this book that you have more ability to be in contact with the different parts of yourself. You will likely have felt increased self-worth and confidence and feel calmer. You may have grown in compassion for yourself and your anxious parts and feel more in touch and able to express your authentic self.

Remember that rewiring takes time. Look for the positive in a relationship rather than focusing on the difficulties. Helping the nervous system to spend more and more time in social engagement is a practice. You are in the process of finding safety inside yourself and in the world. Forming a secure attachment to yourself and others is part of your personal hero's journey.

Please use this book as a resource, refer to it and repeat the exercises as often as you need. If it works best for you, focus on one chapter at a time and use all the resources that I have made available for you online. If you feel that working through this book with a therapist would be helpful, then please seek one out and continue to invest in your healing journey. I am available to work with you through the courses available on my website or in a limited way through one-on-one coaching. Please see my website http://www.psychotherapycentral.health for all my current offerings.

I encourage you to be gentle with yourself when you find yourself in the middle of a protest behavior in the hope of finally being heard or when you notice you have been overly focused on your partner's flaws and dismissing what is wholesome. In those moments, when it is so easy to feel like a failure, invite compassion. Remember how far you have come. Only you can be you, and the world needs you. Now more than ever, the world needs people with the strength to lead with their hearts. Thank you for being on this journey with me, your light has helped me write this book.

All my love, Jen

Acknowledgments

I'd like to thank my ancestors for all they have passed on to me, the struggles and the resources and for surviving the hardships they faced to ensure I am here. Deep gratitude to my mother and father, Janet and Stan, and my grandparents, Joyce and Ernest, for raising me and connecting me intimately with nature.

To all the great teachers and therapists who have taught me directly or indirectly and touched my heart and soul. Some of your light shines through this book.

I'd like to thank the team at New Harbinger Publication for their belief in and support of this project and to Lance, Sheila, Irina, Laura, Jane, and Merle for reviewing elements of the final manuscript and their valuable input. A big thank you to the Psychotherapy Central community, who repeatedly asked for a book on healing anxious attachment. This book exists because of you.

To my children, Isaac and Ariel. Thank you for trusting me with raising and loving you, the most important project of my life. You teach me about attunement, unconditional love, and laughter every day.

Special gratitude to my husband, Lance, for being willing to go deep, for having the love, compassion, and humility to come on this journey of healing and reconnection with me, and for being a loving and attuned secure home base for our children and me. You light up our world.

To all my clients—you give me the opportunity to sit in a field of compassion, kindness, and love and to experience deep healing. In that field, the healing is always for all of us: you, me, our ancestors, and our descendants. We enter into a sacred space in the fullest meaning of the word "sacred," where the heart is touched and moved, where awe lives. Thank you for walking with me. I am eternally grateful.

References

Abraham, E. 2013. "The Magic Question." *The Folio: A Journal for Focusing and Experiential Therapy* 24(1): 1–2.

Anderson, S. E., and R. C. Whitaker. 2011. "Attachment Security and Obesity in US Preschool-Aged Children." *Archives of Pediatrics & Adolescent Medicine* 165: 235–242. https://doi.org/10.1001/arch pediatrics.2010.292.

Berger, R. 2006. "Using Contact with Nature, Creativity, and Ritual as a Therapeutic Medium with Children with Learning Difficulties: A Case Study." *Emotional and Behavioural Difficulties* 11(2): 135–146. https://www.doi.org/10.1080/13632750600619430.

Berger, R. 2008. *Nature Therapy—Developing a Framework for Practice.* Doctoral Thesis. Dundee, UK: University of Abertay.

Berne, E. 1964. *Games People Play: The Basic Handbook of Transactional Analysis.* New York: Ballantine Books.

Boelhouwers, J. 2013. "Meeting Landscape: An Instance at the Seashore." *The Folio: A Journal for Focusing and Experiential Therapy* 24(1): 18–26.

Bowlby, J. 1969. *Attachment and Loss: Volume 1. Attachment.* New York: Basic Books.

———. 1988. *A Secure Base: Parent-Child Attachment and Healthy Human Development.* New York: Basic Books.

Brown, D. P., and D. S. Elliott. 2016. *Attachment Disturbances in Adults: Treatment for Comprehensive Repair.* New York: W. W. Norton & Company.

Campbell, J. 1949. *The Hero with a Thousand Faces.* Novato, CA: New World Library.

Carrère, S., and J. M. Gottman. 1999. "Predicting Divorce Among Newlyweds from the First Three Minutes of a Marital Conflict Discussion." *Family Process* 38(3): 293–301. https://doi.org/10.1111/j .1545-5300.1999.00293.x.

Clifford, A. M. 2021. *Your Guide to Forest Bathing: Experience the Healing Power of Nature*. Newburyport, MA: Red Wheel.

Coan, J. A. 2008. "Toward a Neuroscience of Attachment." In *Handbook of Attachment: Theory, Research, and Clinical Applications*, edited by J. Cassidy and P. R. Shaver (241–265). New York: Guilford Press.

Cozolino, L. 2002. *The Neuroscience of Psychotherapy: Building and Rebuilding the Human Brain*. New York: W. W. Norton & Company.

Dana, D. 2018. *The Polyvagal Theory in Therapy: Engaging the Rhythm of Regulation*. New York: W. W. Norton & Company.

———. 2020. *Polyvagal Exercises for Safety and Connection: 50 Client-Centered Practices*. New York: W. W. Norton & Company.

Egeland, B., D. Jacobvitz, and L. A. Sroufe. 1988. "Breaking the Cycle of Abuse." *Child Development* 59: 1080–1088.

Elkonin, D., O. Brown, and S. Naicker. 2014. "Religion, Spirituality, and Therapy: Implications for Training." *Journal of Religion and Health* 53(1): 119–134. http://www.jstor.org/stable/24485065.

Feeney, J. A. 2016. "Adult Romantic Attachment: Developments in the Study of Couple Relationship." In *Handbook of Attachment: Theory, Research, and Clinical Applications*, edited by J. Cassidy and P. R. Shaver. New York: Guilford Press.

Fraley, R. C., N. G. Waller, and K. A. Brennan. 2000. "An Item-Response Theory Analysis of Self-Report Measures of Adult Attachment." *Journal of Personality and Social Psychology* 78: 350–365.

Fredrickson, B. L., M. A. Cohn, K. A. Coffey, J. Pek, and S. M. Finkel. 2008. "Open Hearts Build Lives: Positive Emotions, Induced Through Loving-Kindness Meditation, Build Consequential Personal Resources." *Journal of Personality and Social Psychology* 95(5): 1045–1062. https://doi.org/10.1037/a0013262.

Fuller, R. A., K. N. Irvine, P. Devine-Wright, P. H. Warren, and K. J. Gaston. 2007. "Psychological Benefits of Greenspace Increase with Biodiversity." *Biology Letters* 3(4): 390–394. https://doi.org/10.1098/rsbl.2007.0149.

Gelsthorpe, J. 2017. "Disconnect from Nature and Its Effect on Health and Well-Being: A Public Engagement Literature Review." *Natural History Museum, Learning and Audience Research Department*. http://www.nhm.ac.uk/content/dam/nhmwww/about-us/visitor-research/Disconnect%20with%20nature%20Lit%20review.pdf.

Gendlin, E. T. 1964. "A Theory of Personality Change." In *Personality Change*, edited by P. Worchel and D. Byrne. New York: John Wiley & Sons.

———. 1978. *Focusing*. New York: Bantam Books.

Gilbert, P. 2009. *The Compassionate Mind*. London, UK: Constable & Robinson.

Grafanaki, S. 2013. "Transformational Focusing: A Journey to Creativity and Discovery of the Inner Poet." *The Folio: A Journal for Focusing and Experiential Therapy* 24(1): 89–92.

Grof, S. 2003. "Technologies of the Sacred, Part Three." *International Journal of Humanities and Peace* 19(1): 104–106.

Hazan, C., and P. Shaver. 1987. "Romantic Love Conceptualized as an Attachment Process." *Journal of Personality and Social Psychology* 52: 511–524.

Heller, D. P. 2019. *The Power of Attachment: How to Create Deep and Lasting Intimate Relationships*. Boulder, CO: Sounds True.

Herbine-Blank, T., D. M. Kerpelman, and M. Sweezy. 2016. *Intimacy from the Inside Out: Courage and Compassion in Couple Therapy*. New York: Routledge.

Hölzel, B. K., J. Carmody, K. C. Evans, E. A. Hoge, J. A. Dusek, L. Morgan, R. K. Pitman, and S. W. Lazar. 2010. "Stress Reduction Correlates with Structural Changes in the Amygdala." *Social Cognitive and Affective Neuroscience* 5(1): 11–17. https://doi.org/10.1093/scan/nsp034.

Hudson, N. W., W. J. Chopik, and D. A. Briley. 2020. "Volitional Change in Adult Attachment: Can People Who Want to Become Less Anxious and Avoidant Move Closer Towards Realizing Those Goals?" *European Journal of Personality* 34(1): 93–114. https://doi.org/10.1002/per.2226.

Jeste, D. V., E. E. Lee, and S. Cacioppo. 2020. "Battling the Modern Behavioral Epidemic of Loneliness: Suggestions for Research and Interventions." *JAMA Psychiatry* 77(6): 553–554. https://doi.org/10.1001/jamapsychiatry.2020.0027.

Johnson, S. M. 2008. *Hold Me Tight: Your Guide to the Most Successful Approach to Building Loving Relationships*. London, UK: Piatkus.

———. 2019. *Attachment Theory in Practice: Emotionally Focused Therapy (EFT) with Individuals, Couples, and Families*. New York: Guilford Press.

Kallos-Lilly, V., and J. Fitzgerald. 2022. *An Emotionally Focused Workbook for Couples: The Two of Us.* London, UK: Routledge.

Kasser, T., and A. Ahuvia. 2002. "Materialistic Values and Well-Being in Business Students." *European Journal of Social Psychology* 32(1): 137–146.

Kasser, T., and R. M. Ryan. 1996. "Further Examining the American Dream: Differential Correlates of Intrinsic and Extrinsic Goals." *Personality and Social Psychology Bulletin* 22(3): 280–287. https://doi.org/10.1177/0146167296223006.

Kok, B., and B. Fredrickson. 2010. "Upward Spirals of the Heart: Autonomic Flexibility, as Indexed by Vagal Tone, Reciprocally and Prospectively Predicts Positive Emotions and Social Connectedness." *Biological Psychology* 85: 432–436. http://doi.org/10.1016/j.biopsycho.2010.09.005.

Konrath, S. H., W. J. Chopik, C. K. Hsing, and E. O'Brien. 2014. "Changes in Adult Attachment Styles in American College Students Over Time: A Meta-Analysis." *Personality and Social Psychology Review* 18(4): 326–348.

Kornfield, J. 2008. *The Wise Heart: A Guide to the Universal Teachings of Buddhist Psychology.* London, UK: Rider.

Leiberg, S., O. Klimecki, and T. Singer. 2011. "Short-Term Compassion Training Increases Prosocial Behavior in a Newly Developed Prosocial Game." *PLOS ONE* 6(3): e17798. https://doi.org/10.1371/journal.pone.0017798.

Levine, A., and R. S. F. Heller. 2010. *Attached: The New Science of Adult Attachment and How It Can Help You Find—and Keep—Love.* London, UK: Penguin.

Li, Q. 2010. "Effect of Forest Bathing Trips on Human Immune Function." *Environmental Health and Preventive Medicine* 15(1): 9–17. https://doi.org/10.1007/s12199-008-0068-3.

Lieberman, M. D., N. I. Eisenberger, M. J. Crockett, S. M. Tom, J. H. Pfeifer, and B. M. Way. 2007. "Putting Feelings into Words: Affect Labeling Disrupts Amygdala Activity in Response to Affective Stimuli." *Psychological Science* 18(5): 421–428. https://doi.org/10.1111/j.1467-9280.2007.01916.x.

Maté, G., and D. Maté. 2022. *The Myth of Normal: Trauma, Illness, and Healing in a Toxic Culture.* London, UK: Penguin.

McCurdy, J. 2022. *I'm Glad My Mom Died*. New York: Simon & Schuster.

McDaniel, K. 2021. *Mother Hunger: How Adult Daughters Can Understand and Heal from Lost Nurturance, Protection, and Guidance*. Carlsbad, CA: Hay House.

McLeod, J. 2013. *An Introduction to Counselling*. 5th ed. Maidenhead, UK: Open University Press.

Mikulincer, M., and P. R. Shaver. 2016. *Attachment in Adulthood: Structure, Dynamics, and Change*. New York: Guilford Press.

Mikulincer, M., P. R. Shaver, Y. Sapir-Lavid, and N. Avihou-Kanza. 2009. "What's Inside the Minds of Securely and Insecurely Attached People? The Secure-Base Script and Its Associations with Attachment-Style Dimensions." *Journal of Personality and Social Psychology* 97: 615–633. https://doi.org/10.1037/a0015649.

Minuchin, S., and H. C. Fishman. 1981. *Family Therapy Techniques*. Cambridge, MA: Harvard University Press.

Narvaez, D. 2019. *Indigenous Sustainable Wisdom: First-Nation Know-How for Global Flourishing*. New York: Peter Lang.

Nhat Hanh, T. 2013. *The Art of Communicating*. San Francisco, CA: HarperOne.

Ogden, P., and J. Fisher. 2015. *Sensorimotor Psychotherapy: Interventions for Trauma and Attachment*. New York: W. W. Norton & Company.

Ogden, P., K. Minton, and C. Pain. 2006. *Trauma and the Body: A Sensorimotor Approach to Psychotherapy*. New York: W. W. Norton & Company.

Porges, S. W. 1995. "Orienting in a Defensive World: Mammalian Modifications of Our Evolutionary Heritage. A Polyvagal Theory." *Psychophysiology* 32(4): 301–318.

———. 2003. "Social Engagement and Attachment: A Phylogenetic Perspective." *Annals of the New York Academy of Sciences* 1008(1): 31–47.

———. 2004. "Neuroception: A Subconscious System for Detecting Threats and Safety." *Zero to Three* 24(5): 19–24. https://chhs.fresnostate.edu/ccci/documents/07.15.16%20Neuroception%20Porges%202004.pdf.

————. 2017. "The Body's Life-Saving Response to Trauma, with Stephen Porges." *National Institute for the Clinical Application of Health and Medicine.* Youtube video, July 20, https://www.youtube.com/watch?v=8WHqO6wCCEs.

————. 2021. *Polyvagal Safety: Attachment, Communication, Self-Regulation.* New York: W. W. Norton & Company.

Rosenburg, M. B. 2015. *Nonviolent Communication: A Language of Life.* Encinitas, CA: PuddleDancer Press.

Roszak, T. 2001. *The Voice of the Earth: An Exploration of Ecopsychology.* Grand Rapids, MI: Phanes Press.

Schwartz, R. C. 2021. *No Bad Parts: Healing Trauma and Restoring Wholeness with the Internal Family Systems Model.* Boulder, CO: Sounds True.

Sodhi, R. 2014. "Spirituality and Religiosity as Predictors of Mental and Physical Health." *Indian Journal of Health and Wellbeing* 5(2): 273–278.

Stanley, E. A. 2019. *Widen the Window: Training Your Brain and Body to Thrive During Stress and Recover from Trauma.* London, UK: Yellow Kite.

Ulsamer, B. 2020. *The Art and Practice of Family Constellations: Leading Family Constellations as Developed by Burt Hellinger.* Independently published.

Waters, H. S., and E. Waters. 2006. "The Attachment Working Models Concept: Among Other Things, We Build Scriptlike Representations of Secure Base Experiences." *Attachment & Human Development* 8: 185–198.

Zeifman, D. M., and C. Hazan. 2016. "Pair Bonds as Attachment: Mounting Evidence in Support of Bowlby's Hypothesis." In *Handbook of Attachment: Theory, Research, and Clinical Applications,* edited by J. Cassidy and P. R. Shaver. New York: Guilford Press.

Jennifer Nurick, MA, is a licensed clinical psychotherapist, energetic healer, author, teacher, and founder of Psychotherapy Central. She specializes in treating people who experience repeating relational issues, as well as those with complex post-traumatic stress disorder (C-PTSD), using traditional psychotherapy approaches and newer body-centered and integrative healing methods Learn more at www.psychotherapycentral .health.

Real change *is* possible

For more than forty-five years, New Harbinger has published proven-effective self-help books and pioneering workbooks to help readers of all ages and backgrounds improve mental health and well-being, and achieve lasting personal growth. In addition, our spirituality books offer profound guidance for deepening awareness and cultivating healing, self-discovery, and fulfillment.

Founded by psychologist Matthew McKay and Patrick Fanning, New Harbinger is proud to be an independent, employee-owned company. Our books reflect our core values of integrity, innovation, commitment, sustainability, compassion, and trust. Written by leaders in the field and recommended by therapists worldwide, New Harbinger books are practical, accessible, and provide real tools for real change.

newharbingerpublications

MORE BOOKS from
NEW HARBINGER PUBLICATIONS

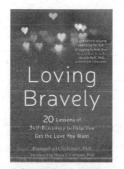
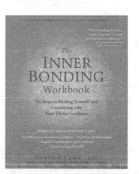

Did you know there are **free tools** you can download for this book?

Free tools are things like **worksheets**, **guided meditation exercises**, and **more** that will help you get the most out of your book.

You can download free tools for this book—whether you bought or borrowed it, in any format, from any source—from the New Harbinger website. All you need is a NewHarbinger.com account. Just use the URL provided in this book to view the free tools that are available for it. Then, click on the "download" button for the free tool you want, and follow the prompts that appear to log in to your NewHarbinger.com account and download the material.

You can also save the free tools for this book to your **Free Tools Library** so you can access them again anytime, just by logging in to your account! Just look for this button on the book's free tools page.

+ Save this to my free tools library

If you need help accessing or downloading free tools, visit **newharbinger.com/faq** or contact us at **customerservice@newharbinger.com**.